THE HEBREW PROPHETS

A STORY-WORKBOOK

written and illustrated by

CHAYA M. BURSTEIN

UAHC PRESS

New York, New York

This book is dedicated to all of us–children and heirs of the Prophets and of the Great Assembly–who try to live by their standards.

Moses received the Torah from Sinai and handed it on to Joshua,
and Joshua to the Elders, and the Elders to the Prophets,
and the Prophets handed it on to the Men of the Great Assembly.

Talmud

Copyright © 1990 by Chaya M. Burstein
Manufactured in the United States of America
10 9 8 7 6 5 4 3 2 1

CONTENTS

ABOUT THE HEBREW PROPHETS   4

ABOUT THE BIBLE   5

1   MOSES
March into the Desert   6

2   DVORA
The Chariots of Yavin   18

3   SAMUEL
Alone in the Sanctuary   28

4   ELIJAH
Murderer in the Vineyard   37

5   ISAIAH
Wolves and Lambs   46

6   JEREMIAH
Which Side Are You On?   55

7   EZEKIEL
The Best Show in Town   64

8   A LIGHT UNTO THE NATIONS   73

9   THEN AND NOW   76

WORKBOOK ANSWERS   80

DATES   80

ABOUT THE HEBREW PROPHETS

Moses, the first and greatest Hebrew prophet, did magic tricks. He turned his walking stick into a snake, made water spurt from solid rock, and moved an entire sea out of its bed. But that doesn't explain the meaning of a prophet. The prophets were much more than magicians.

Elijah, another prophet, was a healer who made a dead child come back to life. But the prophets were much more than healers or doctors.

The prophets Micah, Isaiah, and Jeremiah could see into the future. They predicted famines, earthquakes, and wars. But the prophets were more than seers or fortune-tellers.

So what were they?

Prophets were people who felt they had a direct phone line to heaven. Their every deed and word was at God's direction. With God's help they looked at the world around them, a world of kings, queens, priests, slaves, the very rich and the very poor, and they saw clearly the bad things that were happening. Then they explained what was right and wrong to anybody who would listen. If nobody listened, they pounded on the table, shouted, jumped up and down, and made trouble. They simply would not accept injustice–even if the king himself was the evildoer. The prophets risked being thrown into prison or even being killed because they believed God was speaking through them to teach the Jewish people to obey God's laws.

So what were the prophets? They were teachers. They lived more than twenty-five centuries ago when the Jewish people were becoming a new, young nation settling into their own land. The prophets taught all the people of Israel–from kings to the simplest farmers. For a textbook they used the words of the Hebrew Bible. And they received their instructions right from the principal's office–from God.

To begin to understand the prophets we need to know something about their textbook, the Bible.

ABOUT THE BIBLE

Every Saturday morning the ark in the synagogue is opened and the Hebrew Torah, the first five books of the Bible, is taken out to be read. It is a long parchment scroll rolled onto two rods. The scroll usually wears a brightly embroidered velvet robe with silver or gold decorations. The rods are topped by silver crowns and tiny jingling silver bells.

Jews dress up their Torah because they honor and love it. Its laws teach the Jewish people how to live. And its stories are like a map that shows where the Jewish people came from and serves as a trail guide for the road ahead. Most of the later holy books of the Bible are based on the Torah, and most Jewish holidays and customs grow from it.

The three main parts of the Bible are called Torah, Prophets, and Writings. In Hebrew the names are Torah, Neviim, and Ketuvim. The Hebrew name for all three parts of the Bible–Tanach–is composed of the first letter of each Hebrew name.

Every Shabbat of the year we read a section of the Torah scroll. We also read a chapter of the second part of the Bible–the Prophets, or Neviim. This special added reading is called the Haftarah. When boys and girls are called to the Torah to become a Bar or Bat Mitzvah they also read the Haftarah portion. The words of the prophets have been a special Shabbat treat in synagogues for many centuries.

The stories in this book tell about the prophets, how they lived, and what they said. Their words were written more than 2,500 years ago when people prayed to idols, fought with spears and arrows, and rode in chariots. Do they make sense in our world of computers, robots, and *Star-Wars* weapons? Read and see.

1. MOSES

Setting the stage for Moses, the first prophet...

"In the beginning God created the heaven and the earth...." That's how the Torah begins. It tells about the beginning of the world, about Adam and Eve, the great Flood, the Tower of Babel, and many more stories. Then the Torah begins to concentrate on the history of the Jewish people. This is what it tells:

Abraham and Sarah were the first Jews. God made an agreement, a berit, with Abraham and promised to give the Land of Israel to him and to his descendants. So Abraham, Sarah, and their household left their home in Mesopotamia and came to live in the Promised Land. Abraham's great-grandson, Joseph, was kidnapped and carried away from Israel to Egypt. Later Joseph's father, his brothers, and their families moved to Egypt, too. The families grew into twelve large tribes and lived peacefully in the land of Egypt. After many years the pharaoh of Egypt began to enslave the Hebrew tribes. Then God called on Moses, the first Hebrew prophet, and ordered him to force Pharaoh to free the Jews. Once the slaves were free, he was to gather them together and lead them out of Egypt and back to the Promised Land. This turned out to be a much harder job than Moses had expected.

MARCH INTO THE DESERT

The shouting and pounding on the door of her small, mud-walled house woke Nadiva.

"Moses, go to the pharaoh's palace immediately!"

From the opposite side of the bedroom Nadiva heard Moses, their visitor from the desert, jump up from his bed mat. He tiptoed across the sleeping family and then tripped over Nadiva's feet.

"Ouch!" she yelped.

"Sorry," Moses whispered, and ran out the door and up the narrow lane.

Nadiva rubbed her ankle and blinked back quick tears. Stop crying, she told herself. Do you want Papa to call you a crybaby again? It's only a little bump. She sniffled and tried to think of something interesting instead. And the first thing she thought of was Moses, the strange guest who had come to them out of the desert, bringing a thrilling message. And I was the first one to know about him, she thought proudly. She remembered exactly the day when it happened. She had been sent to bring water to the Hebrew slaves who were building a new palace for Pharaoh. The jug was full and very heavy, and as she walked water splashed out. "Stupid Hebrew!" shouted one of the Egyptian guards. He lashed at her with his whip. She jumped back, the jug tipped off her shoulder, and all the water spilled out. The guard yelled and cursed and swung his whip. The thirsty slaves scolded her, too. And Nadiva ran back to the well gulping tears, her back stinging.

A tall, hawk-nosed man with a wiry gray beard was hauling water up from the well. He looked at her grimy, unhappy face and without a word took the jug from her and began to fill it. This quiet sympathy was too much–Nadiva burst out crying. "Why is the guard so mean... just because we're slaves?... I tried so hard.... It was too heavy," she sobbed.

The man finished filling the jar. "It's hard to be a slave, isn't it?" he said. With the corner of his robe he dried her tears. "You won't be a slave much longer," he continued. "God has sent me to free the Hebrew people."

"Nobody can free us. Pharaoh won't let them." She began to sniffle again, and then she looked up curiously. "God? What God?" she asked.

"The God of all creation. The God of the Hebrews."

"I didn't know slaves could have their own god," said Nadiva with surprise. "Is this one as strong as the sun or the moon, like the god of the Egyptians?"

The man smiled. "Our God *made* the sun and the moon and everything else. So of course our God has power over everything. And our God is everyplace–in the heavens, in the flowers and trees and bushes. Even inside you and me."

"Inside me?" Nadiva looked down at her sturdy ten-year-old body with wonder. "Wow." She pulled back her shoulders proudly without even noticing the sting and took a deep breath. Then she got worried again. "How do you know?" she asked.

The stranger's eyes glowed brightly out of his sun-bronzed face like the coals of a campfire in the night, and he said, "I saw God. We spoke to each other. And God promised me my people would go free. Now go back to work. The laborers are waiting for water."

By the next day all the Hebrew slaves knew about Moses. But not all of them were happy with his promise of freedom. Nadiva's father said, "What's this silliness about freedom? Freedom could mean misery.

Better the misery that I know here in Egypt than a misery I don't know." But nothing could stop Moses. He marched to the royal palace and demanded that Pharaoh free the Hebrew slaves. When Pharaoh laughed at him and refused, God began to punish the land of Egypt.

Nadiva clucked softly, lying on her mat, as she remembered the nine terrible plagues God had sent. Suddenly Nadiva had an idea that was so exciting, she nearly flew out of bed. Maybe the plagues finally forced Pharaoh to change his mind, she thought. Maybe that's why he summoned Moses in the middle of the night–to tell him he was ready to set the Hebrews free!

"That Moses," her father mumbled sleepily in the darkness. "Who needs him? I haven't had a decent night's sleep since he came to stay in this house. Day and night, meetings and messengers and talk, talk, talk.... I wish he'd go back to the desert."

"He came because God sent him, Papa," said Nadiva. "He's going to make Pharaoh set us free."

"What do you understand, child? You're only ten years old. The man is a fool! He wants to take us out of Egypt and drop us in the middle of the desert. Do you know what's in the desert? Poisonous snakes, lions, leopards, criminals, bandits! They'll tear us to pieces."

"I do too understand!" she burst out with an insulted sob.

"Stop crying," he said. "And stop arguing."

Nadiva's mother hushed them both. "You'll wake up the whole neighborhood. Get some sleep. It's the middle of the night."

The house grew quiet again. But Nadiva couldn't sleep. *I do understand, even if I'm just ten and I cry a lot. Moses said our God is the only real God in the world. And our God is strong enough and smart enough to save us from lions and bandits. I'm not one bit scared.*

But a second later she nearly jumped out of her skin as an eerie wail rose from the dark houses of the Egyptians across the lane.

"Aaaaaiiieeeee.... Oh, my son, my son!"

Nadiva wiggled to the doorway and peeked out. An oil lamp flickered in their neighbor's window. More wails and sobs burst from open windows nearby. "My child is dead! My son!" More lights were lit.

Then Nadiva remembered that after Pharaoh's last refusal to free the Hebrews Moses had warned him the firstborn son of each Egyptian family would die. It would be God's punishment. In spite of the warning Pharaoh would not free the Hebrews. And now the warning was coming true. The tenth plague was hitting the Egyptians. Their firstborn sons were dying!

The crying grew louder. Nadiva put her fingers in her ears, but that didn't help. Then footsteps pounded down the lane. Torches flamed, and hoarse voices shouted, "Weep, Egyptians. The Pharaoh's firstborn son is dead!" The wailing from the Egyptian houses became howls of despair.

Nadiva shrank back from the doorway. Her eyes filled with tears again. "Poor, poor Egyptian parents; poor little boys," she whispered.

Suddenly, in the middle of the crying, a different voice rang out with a joyous shout. "People of Israel, arise! Pack up your things!"

Nadiva scrambled back to the doorway. Far up the lane, running from the direction of the palace, she saw a tall, white-robed man with a gray jutting beard. He was carrying a torch high in one hand and banging on the shutters of Israelite houses with the stick in his other hand. It was Moses.

His strong voice cut through the wailing and the sobs. "Get up, Israelites. Hurry. Pharaoh has bowed to God. He is allowing you to go free."

Nadiva quickly wiped her tears. "Get up, Mama, Papa!" She shook the grown-ups and jumped on her younger brothers. "We're free. We're leaving!"

Men, women, and children tumbled from their sleeping mats all through the Israelite quarter. They ran around collecting food, filling goatskins with water, loading the donkeys, and stuffing squawking chickens into wicker cages. Babies cried and crawled underfoot. Children raced from house to house on errands, bumping into one another excitedly.

When the sky was brightening in the east, loaded donkeys and carts and eager people crowded the narrow lanes of the Israelite section of the town. Moses climbed onto a cart so everybody could see him. His sister, Miriam, and brother, Aaron, stood close beside him. "Brothers and sisters, follow me to the land God has promised us," he cried.

"To the Promised Land!" people shouted, and pushed forward.

"To be free!" Nadiva laughed. "No more carrying water for the Egyptians."

Free? Nadiva's parents looked anxiously at each other. But they were pushed along by their neighbors and quickly gathered up their bundles.

The road was dewy under Nadiva's bare feet, and morning mist clouded the fields as the Hebrews moved away from their homes. Some sang and looked ahead with shining eyes. But some, like Nadiva's mother and father, looked back. "Where are we going?" they asked. "And why?"

Moses, the strange man from the desert, strode in front of the Israelites. His eyes were shining, too. I finally did it, he thought. I'm leading my people out of slavery. We're going home. He remembered how frightened he had been when God called. He hadn't wanted this job. He had been a shepherd living peacefully with his family and tending his sheep and goats. But God called, and he'd had to come to Egypt. And now he was a shepherd again, a shepherd for his people. "God," he whispered. "Please help me to lead the Hebrews and teach them to live by Your laws."

The long line of people and animals moved south at first and then turned east toward the Sinai Desert. Some of the Hebrews remembered the old stories of the land of Canaan. It was the land their forebears had come from. It's a beautiful, green country on the other side of the desert," they said.

"How far?" asked Nadiva's father.

Nobody knew. Nadiva's father shook his head uneasily.

"Papa, really, it's all right. I trust Moses," said Nadiva.

"Just because *you* trust Moses you think *I* should trust him? What makes you an expert?"

"He says God is with us."

"What God? Who is this God? Has anyone seen this God?"

"Moses saw God," Nadiva insisted.

Her father clapped his hand to his forehead in disgust and turned away.

Soon Nadiva's brothers and the other children began to complain.

"When will we get there? I'm tired."

"My tooth hurts from walking."

"I have a blister–a giant one!"

"I have a stomachache. I think I need to throw up."

"Are we there yet?"

The complaints got louder and louder as the Hebrews went on. Moses pressed his lips tightly together, and the happy light left his eyes. Nadiva ran forward to walk beside him. "It must've been easier to lead goats and sheep than it is to lead us, right?" she said. He smiled down at her and nodded.

One late afternoon the Israelites found themselves struggling along a muddy path between tall reeds. Shore birds flapped overhead, and mosquitoes hummed around their noses. As Nadiva smacked at the mosquitoes she started to worry. Does Moses really know the way to the Promised Land? Just then the leader stopped walking and raised his arms high. The people, donkeys, goats, sheep, children, and all their bundles piled up around him in a pushing, shoving mass. But as they looked ahead they pulled back and grew quiet.

A great mist-covered, swampy sea bristling with reeds stretched in front of them.

The Israelites looked at the sea, and then they turned to look at Moses, afraid of what he would tell them to do.

"We must go forward into the sea," said Moses.

Everybody started screaming and crying at once: "I can't swim.

We'll be food for the fishes! Get a boat! Does he think we can walk on water? I want to go home to Egypt!"

And, as if that weren't bad enough, a terrified howl suddenly rose from the back of the great crowd. "The Egyptians are coming!"

In the hush that followed, the Israelites heard the faraway rumble of heavy war chariots. The mud trembled under their feet, and a cloud of yellow dust rose far back on the road they had been following.

The crying and sobbing broke out again, but much louder: "We're trapped! We'll drown in the sea, or the pharaoh will slaughter us! We should have stayed as slaves! Moses, Moses, why did you do this to us!"

Moses raised his arms again and waited for quiet. His face was sad, but his beard jutted out stubbornly.

He's sad because we're frightened, because we don't trust him or God, Nadiva thought. She took a deep breath and called out, "We're with you, Moses. Just tell us what to do."

The grown-ups around Nadiva frowned at her, but Moses' eyes twinkled, and his chin rose even higher. "Trust God," he roared over the wailing of the people. "Do not be afraid. God will fight for you, and you will be safe!" Then his face seemed to close, and he turned away and looked up to the purple sunset sky.

As the people waited, shivering, dark clouds rolled in over the water and dropped like a curtain between the Hebrews and the oncoming Egyptians. Moses raised his staff and stretched it out over the Sea of Reeds. A fierce wind began to blow from the east, tearing at the reeds and at the clothing and hair of the Israelites. The mist peeled up from the water, and waves tossed and foamed.

Nadiva gasped as the spray hit her face. Her little brother began to howl and kick in the sling on her back. She didn't hear him. She was watching the sea, not believing what she saw. The wind was driving the water back into two heaving, churning walls, and a space was being cleared between the walls. As the sun set and the first stars glimmered, a bare, dry path appeared on the sea bottom.

Moses stepped down onto the path. One young man followed him. Everybody else stood frozen, staring at the foaming walls. Nadiva looked back to her frightened parents and then to Moses. She had to choose! "Mama, Papa, please come!" she cried as she slid down the bank to the sea bottom carrying her brother along. With a sob her mother rushed after her. The rest of the family and all the Israelite families and all

their belongings, sheep, goats, donkeys, cats, and dogs came pouring down onto the path behind them.

They hurried through the night while the howling wind tore at them and fought back the angry water. As they reached the eastern shore they heard rumbling, shouts, and clashing weapons behind them. On the faraway bank moonlight sparkled on swords and helmets. Yelling fiercely, blowing battle horns, and waving their swords, the Egyptian army, led by Pharaoh himself, galloped down onto the seabed and rushed after the Hebrews along the path between the waters.

The last of the Hebrews ran to reach the bank. Strong arms pulled them up to safety as dawn brightened the sky. Then Moses walked slowly to the edge of the bank, raised his staff, and stretched it out over the seabed. The wind slowed and died and, as the sun moved higher in the sky, the water tumbled back into the dry bed of the Sea of Reeds. While the Hebrews huddled on the bank and watched, the sea swirled and gurgled around Pharaoh, his chariots, horses, and all of his soldiers. Higher and higher it rose until every Egyptian was swallowed up.

One lone Egyptian spear tossed up and down on the rippling water. Nadiva stared at it, and tears rolled down her cheeks. "How awful . . . all those people and horses," she sobbed. She felt her father's arm on her shoulders and tried to stop crying. Then she looked up and saw with surprise that his eyes, too, were filled with tears.

"It had to happen," he said in a choked voice. "It is a sad, terrible lesson. The Egyptians didn't believe in the power of God. Nor did I. Now I've learned." His hand shook on her shoulder as he went on: "I'm still scared. But I think I'm ready to follow Moses into the desert now."

"Don't cry, Papa," said Nadiva. She pressed close to him, and they watched as the spear sank into the water.

Tambourine bells jingled, and clay drums began to pound. Miriam, the sister of Moses, was leading a happy, stamping dance of thanks to God. Nadiva's mother took her hand and pulled her into the circle of dancing women and girls. "I will sing praises to my God. Sing to God who has thrown the horse and the rider into the sea," they sang.

As Nadiva spun around, the tears dried on her cheeks. She forgot her sadness and sang out as loudly as the others.

Moses stood alone and watched the dancers. He was relieved they were out of Egypt at last. And yet, like Nadiva and her father, he was sad. God must be sad, too, at the deaths of so many living creatures, he thought, and then wondered, Does God cry? He pushed the question aside. There was too much else to worry about. The dry, rocky desert lay ahead of them.

In the midst of the happy celebration Moses spoke silently to God. "O God, how will I do what You ask of me? These are a stiff-necked people. They feel safe now, but tomorrow they'll be miserable and frightened again. How will I teach them to believe in You and obey You? How will I tie them together in one united people?"

Moses felt his stomach clench with fear as he turned away to face the waiting desert. Nadiva whirled past in the circle, but she didn't notice the lonely figure. She was happy again, too happy to worry about tomorrow.

The Hebrews stood on the riverbank and laughed and danced and sang to God who had rescued them from Pharaoh. Then Moses led them on into the desert. At Mount Sinai, deep in the stony wilderness, they waited, frightened and awestruck, as God spoke to them out of a cloud. Moses went up into the cloud and later came down bringing the Ten Commandments and many other laws of the Jewish religion.

"All the words God has said we will do!" cried the people. And they really meant it ... at least for a while. They built an ark to hold the Commandments, then packed up again and moved on. For forty years the Hebrews wandered in the desert. They soon forgot their promise and began to argue and complain again, giving Moses a forty-year headache, until ... by the end of the wandering they had learned to be a strong, united people who believed in God and tried to follow the Commandments.

Moses was a hundred and twenty years old by the time he brought his people to the border of the Promised Land. Before he died he chose Joshua to lead the tribes across the Jordan River into the Land of Israel.

Here's what happened next....

Writings

Without Moses and the forty years of wandering and learning in the desert, the Hebrew tribes might never have become a united people, and the long history of the Jews might never have happened.

The Torah remembers the great leader with awe:

> A prophet like Moses never arose again in Israel,
> Moses, whom the Lord knew face to face.
>
> Deuteronomy 34:10

Through Moses God gave this promise and warning to the people of Israel:

> You shall observe all the commandments which I command you this day, so that you may live and multiply and go in and possess the land which God promised to your fathers....

> For the Lord brings you into a good land of brooks of water ... a land of wheat and barley, and vines and fig trees and pomegranates, a land of olive trees and honey.... But if you forget ... your God, who brought you out of Egypt, who led you through the dreadful wilderness ... if you walk after other gods and serve them and worship them, I warn you this day that you will surely perish.
>
> Deuteronomy 8:1-19

> I have set before you life and death, the blessing and the curse. Therefore choose life, that you may live, you and your children.
>
> Deuteronomy 30:19

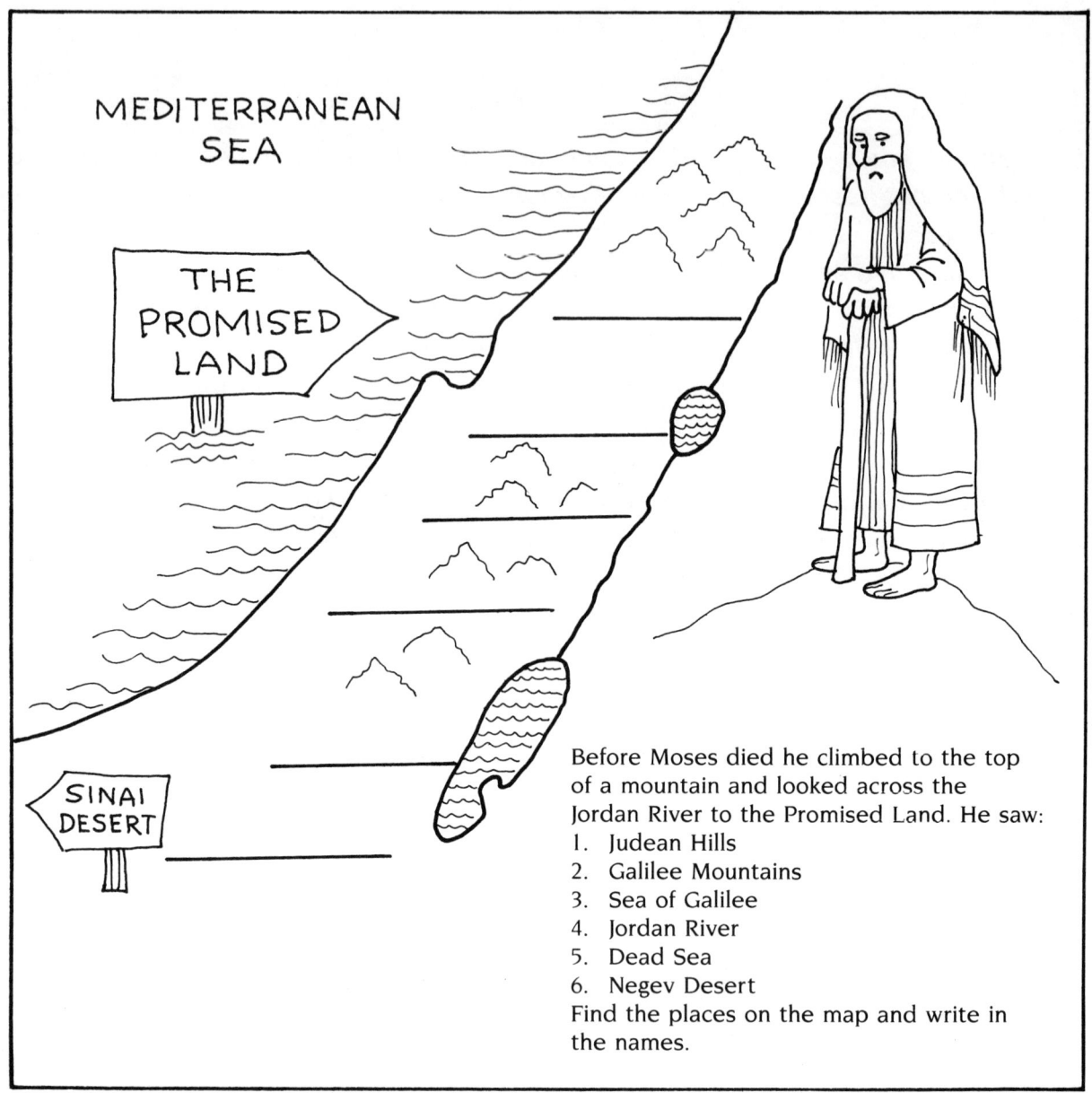

Before Moses died he climbed to the top of a mountain and looked across the Jordan River to the Promised Land. He saw:
1. Judean Hills
2. Galilee Mountains
3. Sea of Galilee
4. Jordan River
5. Dead Sea
6. Negev Desert

Find the places on the map and write in the names.

DESERT LESSONS

What were the most important things God and Moses did in the desert to turn the Hebrew tribes into a strong people? Number them in order of importance. Cross out lines that don't belong.
- Taught them to be good hikers and swimmers.
- Brought them the Torah with its laws of the Jewish religion.
- Drowned the Egyptians.
- Led them to the Land of Israel.
- Taught them to walk through water without getting wet.
- Appointed a king to rule them.
- Freed them from working hard.
- Taught them to trust and believe in God.

Pretend you and your classmates are slaves in Egypt. Choose one student to be Moses and another to be a Hebrew slave leader who is against the Exodus. Let them argue about whether to stay or leave. Then have the slaves (the class) vote on which leader to follow.

Rearrange these letters to spell the names of the three books of the Torah.
1. ROAHT

   _ _ _ _ _

2. EHPOSTRP

   _ _ _ _ _ _ _ _

3. NITWIRGS

   _ _ _ _ _ _ _ _

Now can you do it in Hebrew?

1. הרתו

   _ _ _ _ _

2. בינאמי

   _ _ _ _ _ _

3. תיכובם

   _ _ _ _ _ _

Check your answers on page 80.

Black slaves who were converted to Christianity loved Bible stories. They told the stories in songs called "spirituals," which gave them hope and courage to face their hard lives. "Go Down, Moses" is the name of a spiritual. Another one is "Dem Bones." It tells about Ezekiel's prophecy. Find it in Chapter Seven.

2. DVORA

The story goes on....

THE CHARIOTS OF YAVIN

The second book of the Bible–Neviim, or Prophets–describes a big change in the lives of the Hebrew people. Here's what happened:

The tribes of Israel stormed across the Jordan River into the Promised Land, which was called Canaan at that time. They began to conquer the cities and take over as much land as they could. After the conquered land was divided among the twelve Hebrew tribes, they stopped wandering and settled down to build villages and become farmers, shepherds, and craftsmen. Each tribe chose judges to settle arguments between people and to make rules. And at the town of Shiloh the Hebrews built a temple to house the Ark of the Covenant, or Berit. Priests from the tribe of Levi led the prayers and took care of the sacrifices offered to God at the temple.

That was when new troubles started. As soon as the Hebrews became a settled people with property and land, other people began to attack and rob them.

The twelve tribes weren't united, as they had been under the leadership of Moses and Joshua. Enemies like the Canaanites and the Philistines could attack one tribe at a time and steal cattle, burn houses, and take captives. Now and then a strong leader would pull a few tribes together to fight back and drive out their enemies. Dvora the prophet, judge of the tribes of Zebulun and Naphtali, was that kind of leader.

Dvora the judge was tough. Nothing scared her, and she took no nonsense from anybody... except her six grandchildren. Each day she sat under her palm tree on Mount Ephraim while thieves and other law breakers were brought before her to be judged. Sometimes quarreling villagers came, shouting and shoving one another. Dvora listened closely to each person. When she had heard enough, she raised her hand and stared down at the arguer with her black brows drawn close over her piercing eyes. He gulped his final words and shrank down on his stool. Then, with a thump of her stick, Dvora announced her judgment.

But with her grandchildren Dvora was as soft as potter's clay. Even after a day of hard listening she loved to sit in the courtyard and play with the little ones or talk to Uri, the oldest, who wanted to be a judge when he grew up. When there was no judging to do, they walked together in the fields and collected flowers or mint for tea. And later she baked flat honey cakes for the children in her earthen oven.

Being busy with law breakers, quarreling villagers, or grandchildren, Dvora almost never found time to be alone. But late one night she felt very much alone. After tossing and turning on her bed mat while Lapidot, her husband, snored beside her, Dvora got up and tiptoed out the door. She needed to walk on the mountain, to think and worry and talk to God. She had a decision to make–such an important decision, she could not make it by herself.

That day a tired, dust-covered messenger had arrived from the north. He told of the troubles the Israelite tribes were having with the Canaanite king, Yavin of Hatzor. Canaanite soldiers were stealing crops from the fields, blocking the roads, and snatching people away to use them as slaves. The Israelites were so frightened, they had run away from their fields and villages and huddled together in the larger towns. "Brother and sister Israelites, come to help us drive out the Canaanites!" the messenger pleaded.

Yavin the Canaanite filled Dvora's mind as she climbed the narrow mountain path in the middle of the night. "What to do, what to do?" she puzzled. Brambles tore at her robe. In the dim starlight she stumbled over piles of earth rooted up by wild boars. She could hear them grunting and snuffling in the undergrowth. But the boars didn't scare her. Only Yavin scared her.

Dvora pushed ahead through the brush until she reached the highest spot on the mountain, where a mound of rocks poked at the sky. She stopped and took deep breaths of the spicy air, fragrant with oak leaves. Some place on the next hill a jackal howled. Another answered with a sad, wailing cry. The valley below was a crisscross of mist-covered fields and terraces separated by the silvery crowns of olive trees.

I love this hill and these fields, she thought. I want to be buried here. I want my children and grandchildren to plant sunflowers and wheat here and to grow and raise their families here. Why should I send them off to war to help a faraway tribe? And if I send them, and if we lose, then Yavin will be our enemy forever. She shivered as the dew began to soak through her robe and chill her skin. But the argument in her head

kept going. We are one people. God gave this land to all of us. We have to help our brothers and sisters. And if we don't help them now, the Canaanites will come to our land one day, and then who will help *us*?

Dvora looked across the hills, far to the north. Round Mount Tabor loomed faintly in the starlight. That's how the Canaanites will come, she thought, from the north. They'll roll over our fields in their iron chariots and burn our houses and steal our children.... She could feel tears burning her eyes, but she rubbed them off angrily. I have no time to cry. I have to decide. But I can't.... I need help.

Her eyes searched the clear, starry sky. "God, God of Israel," she cried, "help me decide. I'm so mixed up. What should I tell my people?"

The jackal howled again, but the stars were silent. From the village a donkey brayed faintly. Mist began to blow across the path, and Dovra's shoulders ached with the dampness. She waited, but there was no answer. Finally, sadly, she folded her arms tight across her chest, tucked in her chin, and began to push her way back through the bushes.

A sudden new sound made her stop. A murmur was rising from the misty path ahead.

Out of the swirling wisps of fog she heard a voice.
> RAISE AN ARMY OF ISRAELITES AGAINST SISERA. BRING HIM TO THE KISHON, TO MOUNT TABOR. THERE YOU WILL DEFEAT HIM!

Dvora waited, holding her breath and staring into the fog. The mist swirled emptily. The voice did not speak again. But it was enough. Her aches and fears were gone. She wanted to laugh and cry and sing all at once. "Thank You, God," she cried, flinging up her arms. "I've heard Your words. I'll do as You say!"

Dvora went crashing wildly through the bushes and over the rocks, back to the village. She burst through the doorway panting and yelling, "Lapidot, wake up! God spoke to me!"

"Wha-what–it's the middle of the night," her husband protested sleepily.

"Listen to me!" she said, fixing him with her fiercest "judge" stare. "God spoke to me from the mist and said we must rally the tribes. We must fight Sisera, Yavin's general."

Lapidot sat up. He knew his wife. She was tough. If the mist spoke to Dovra in the voice of God, Lapidot knew better than to try to sleep. "All right. I hear you," he grunted. "We'll call Barak of Kedesh in Naphtali. He is our best fighting man. May God be with us and with him. Now let me warm your feet before you catch cold."

Barak came striding up the hill a few days later. He was tall, bronze-skinned, and broad-shouldered, with a black beard as thick as a bramble bush. Two boys followed, carrying his heavy shield, spear, and sword. The children of the village gathered around and timidly touched the sword's carved holster. Uri was so impressed, he began to think he might want to be a general when he grew up instead of a judge.

"*Shalom aleichem*," Barak's voice boomed out as he greeted the townspeople with a smile. But his eyes did not smile. They were wary and anxious. As soon as he and Dvora sat alone together in her small house, the smile disappeared.

"We can't fight Sisera," he blurted. "We're too weak."

"We can!" Dvora snapped back. "God told me we can."

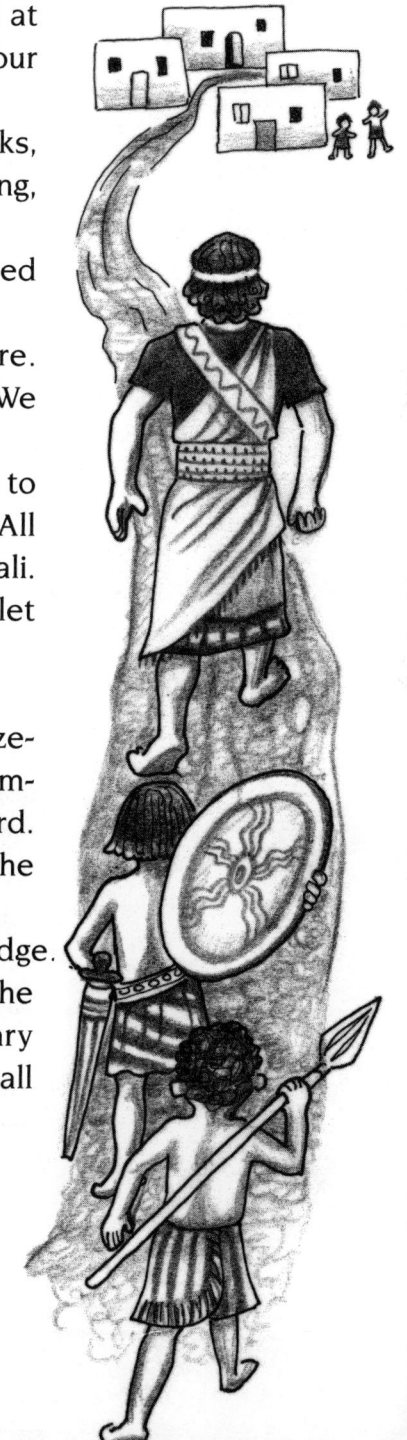

21

Barak clenched his big fists. "Be realistic," he said. "We don't have a single chariot. The Canaanites have nine hundred iron chariots. We don't have enough fighting men or enough weapons. The other Israelite tribes won't help us. We don't–"

"We'll make them help us," Dvora interrupted him. "All the tribes are part of one people. We will stand together. And God will be with us. What more do we need?"

Barak chewed his lip and stared down at his sandals. Then he said, "I can't do it alone. Dvora, come with me."

"Me?" Dvora stared at him. "A grandmother! What do I know about fighting? I raise my stick only when I announce a judgment or when I'm chasing the goats out of my vegetable patch."

"I need you. I don't know how to beat the Canaanites."

"God will tell you how!"

"No," Barak insisted firmly, "God will tell *you*. Without you beside me I can't do it."

"All right." Dvora waved her hand impatiently. "I'll come to Mount Tabor with you. But because you're afraid, you won't be the one to kill Sisera. A woman will do the job."

Barak's face grew red under the tan. "So be it," he said quietly.

In the next few weeks Dvora's messengers hurried over secret paths and trails to all the tribes of Israel. The tribes who were farthest away turned down Dvora's call for help. "This isn't our fight," they answered.

"How can they say that?" Dvora raged. "God commands us to fight for our land as one people. No tribe can ignore the need of another." She stamped angrily around the hilltop and nobody, not even Uri, dared talk to her. She sent the messengers out again telling of God's promise and carrying her fierce demands for unity. And slowly, village by village, the fighters began to come. Farmers and shepherds from the Hebrew tribes of Zebulun, Naphtali, Issachar, Ephraim, and Benjamin dropped their tools, kissed their families goodbye, and came to join Barak and Dvora.

"Please, please let me go, too," Uri pleaded when it was time to set up camp on Mount Tabor.

"An army is no place for a child," Dvora said firmly.

"It's no place for a grandma either. You'll need my help to make tea or deliver a message or something. Please."

Dvora laughed. "What an army this will be. With no chariots but with a grandma and a little boy."

"And with God and Barak as the generals," Uri said happily. "We'll win for sure."

News of the uprising soon reached the Canaanite king, Yavin, in his palace in Hazor.

"It's nothing," he sneered. "I'll squash it quickly." He called up his nine hundred iron chariots with their drivers, spearsmen, swordsmen, and archers. With Yavin's general, Sisera, in the lead they came thundering down the flat, green Jordan valley and across to Megiddo.

From high on Mount Tabor the Israelites saw the brown dust rising behind the chariots. As the cloud came closer they heard the pounding of horses' hooves and the screeching and grinding of chariot wheels on the hard-packed earth. Tabor seemed to tremble with the sound of Sisera's great army.

Barak moved back and forth among his fighters giving instructions in a steady voice. Now and then he looked up to where Dvora sat in the shade of a lone carob tree, and then his back straightened and his voice grew stronger. Dvora's cloak was folded double to warm her stiff shoulders, but she held her head high. Her thoughts raced as she spoke silently to God. You said we'd defeat Sisera, and I believe You. I'm not worried at all . . . except maybe a little bit because of Uri. But how will You do it? Really. How? There are so many of them!"

With her eyes fixed on the enemy she hardly noticed the heavy gray clouds rolling up from the western sea.

The line of chariots moved smoothly into a semicircle at the foot of the hill near the brook Kishon. The chariot wheels stopped screeching as Sisera's army settled into position. From above, the Israelites stared down. The Canaanites stared up, with their hands sweating on the

spear shafts and tightly grasping the reins of the nervous, stamping horses. Everybody waited as if frozen. Dvora and Uri sat frozen, too, until Dvora noticed the boy's pale, staring look. "Make a fire for tea," she ordered. He jumped up, shivered, and began to collect twigs.

In the hushed silence the gray clouds swept on until they covered the sky and were only a fingertip from Dvora's hair.

Barak looked up at her. Dvora gritted her teeth. "Now?" she whispered. "Dear God, give me a signal. I don't know what to do." At that moment, with loud plopping sounds, great drops of rain began to fall. Suddenly Dvora was sure. "Now!" she cried. "Now!" She raised her arms high.

Barak lifted his sword in the signal to attack. A hundred priests raised their shofars and blew earsplitting blasts. Drums pounded, trumpets shrilled, and with loud yells the Israelites charged down the rocky slopes.

The drops of rain grew to a torrent that pounded the mountainside and churned the rich brown earth of the valley. In minutes the valley land was a gluey, puddinglike mess. The chariots tried to move forward, but their wheels spun. The horses slipped and skidded. Drivers were tossed into the mud as chariots crashed into one another. Through the hammering rain Israelite arrows came *thwanging*, finding their marks among the confused, struggling Canaanite soldiers. And the water of the brook Kishon began to rise and overflow, turning the mud into a brown soup.

High above on Mount Tabor, the rain swept away Uri's tiny fire for tea. It would have swept Uri down the mountain as well if Dvora hadn't grabbed him. They heard the whinnying of the frightened horses, the screams and trumpeting, the clash of swords against shields in the valley.

"Grandma, I can't see. What's happening?" Uri asked, half sobbing as he wiped rain from his eyes and tried to see the battle. "Who is winning?"

Dvora laughed and hugged him tightly. She raised her face and let the rain pound her nose and cheeks and run down her chin. She drank it in great gulps, as she used to do when she was a little girl. And she felt like a little girl again, safe under God's protection.

"*God* is winning!" she laughed. "God gave us this land and God is helping us to keep it." She raised her hands to the stormy sky and cried, "Praise God, and praise the people of Israel who came willingly to fight for one another!"

Writings

After the battle Dvora sang a victory song. She told the story of Sisera's bloody death and raged against the tribes of Israel who didn't help in the fight. Here are parts of Dvora's song:

> In the time of struggle in Israel when the people came willingly to fight I sing a song to the God of Israel. [O God] when You marched out ... the earth shook and the heavens dripped. Even the clouds dripped water. The mountains melted before ... God ....
> In the days of Yael the highways were empty. Travelers went on back roads, and villagers ran away from their villages. Until I, Dvora, arose ....
> God helped me to unite the people ....
> The stars fought against Sisera. The torrent Kishon swept them away, that ancient brook, the brook of Kishon.
> "Curse those who did not come to help God," said the angel of God.
> Blessed above all women is Yael (when Sisera ran away from the battle he came to Yael's tent). He asked water, and she gave him milk.
> ... She put her hand to the tent peg and the hammer, and she crushed Sisera's temple. He bent, he fell, and lay dead at her feet. The mother of Sisera looked out of the window. "Why is his chariot so long in coming? Why are the hoofbeats of his horses so late?" she wailed. Her wise ladies answered, "They have divided the spoils. To every man a girl or two. To Sisera brightly colored clothing and embroidered fabrics."
> "So, let all Your enemies die, O God. But let those who love You be as strong as the brightest sun."

Based on Judges 5

DVORA'S VICTORY SONG

Read Dvora's victory song.
Find the phrase in the song that comes closest to answering each question.
Write the phrase, or part of it, in the space below the question.

1. In what way did the enemy oppress the Israelites?

2. Did *all* the Hebrew tribes unite to fight Sisera?

3. Was Dvora a proud or a modest person?

4. What spoils would Sisera's victorious soldiers have brought home?

Check your answers on page 80.

WOULD DVORA WIN ANY POPULARITY CONTESTS?

Some sages of the Talmud thought Dvora was too proud and uppity. What do you think?

26

A DVORA CROSSWORD PUZZLE

Across:
2 Israelite general
4 A doctor says, "Open your mouth and say '_____.'"
6 Israelites waited for battle on Mount _____.
8 Alien movie hero
9 Classical composer J. S. _____
11 Canaanite's fighting vehicles
14 Israel's secret weapon
15 Bachelor of Science, abbreviated
16 Sisera's mother felt very _____.
18 Killer of Sisera
19 Negative
20 Dvora's grandson
22 "The _____ is mightier than the sword."

Down:
1 Tree on Mount Tabor
3 Brook that overflowed
4 Past tense of "eat"
5 Enemy's capital city
7 Egyptian sun god
10 Country that was Israel's enemy
12 Resort town in the Sinai Desert
13 Canaanite general
17 First note of the musical scale
20 Canaanites stared _____ at the Israelites.
21 Second note of the musical scale

Check your answers on page 80.

FIGHTING

Dvora thought she had to make war against the Canaanites to protect her people and her land. She must have been right because after the war the Canaanites did not bother the tribes of Israel again. But wars and fighting often do not solve problems. You will read about other prophets who tried to settle disagreements peacefully.

Fights may happen between friends or family members or neighbors.

Tell of three times you had a disagreement or fight at home or at school.

1.

2.

3.

Think of a way you might settle each fight peacefully the next time.

1.

2.

3.

27

3. SAMUEL

The story goes on. . . .

Led by Dvora and other judges the Hebrew tribes kept in touch and sometimes helped one another. They were held together because they shared the Ark of the Berit, where the Ten Commandments were kept, and because they believed in one God, the God of Israel. The ark stood in a temple on the hilltop of Shiloh. People pointed up at the temple with awe. "God lives there," they said. They climbed the hill bringing sacrifices for God and the Levite priests, and then they prayed for help and danced and sang before God. One day a childless woman named Hannah came to pray. She made a promise to God. "If You give me a son, I will give him to You for all the days of his life," she said. A baby boy was born to Hannah. She called him Samuel, and she nursed and hugged and loved him. But she didn't forget her promise. When Samuel was weaned, Hannah brought him to Eli, the high priest at the temple, and left him there.

ALONE IN THE SANCTUARY

Samuel kicked out his legs like one of the guards at the sanctuary and strutted over the hilltop. He felt important. He wasn't just any seven-year-old. He was the high priest's helper. The farmers, shepherds, craftsmen, merchants, and all their children watched him with respect. They had walked for days to come to Shiloh so they could worship God. But he, Samuel son of Hannah and Elkanah, he *lived* here!

"Boy!" A dark-eyed girl tugged at his sash. "Are you a priest?"

She was smaller than he was, so he looked down at her, made his voice as deep as he could, and answered, "Not exactly. But I'm the personal helper of Eli the high priest."

The girl clicked her tongue admiringly. "Did you ever see God's ark in the sanctuary?" she asked. "My mama says it's all covered with gold and it shines."

"Of course I saw it," he said coolly, feeling more important than ever. "I sleep in the room right next to it." He felt a prickle of excitement as he thought of the great battle-scarred ark with two huge winged angel shapes resting on its roof, the ark of Moses, home of the Tablets of the Law, so close beside him.

The girl's eyes opened wide, and her voice dropped to a whisper. "Does God really live there?" she asked. "Did you ever see God?"

He cleared his throat, feeling a little put-down. "Of course God does–some of the time anyhow. But I never saw God. Not even Eli the high priest has seen God."

"Oh." The girl looked disappointed. Then she asked hopefully, "Did you see God's messengers?"

Before Samuel could think of an answer, a woman called to the girl from a cooking fire nearby. "Leave the priest's boy alone, Sarah. He has work to do. Come eat your breakfast. I made fresh pita."

The smell of hot pita topped with fried onions and goat cheese filled the air. Samuel sniffed. It was the same wonderful smell he remembered from home long ago in the town of Ramah. So long ago. He was three years old when his mother, Hannah, brought him here to Shiloh to serve God and Eli. The only thing he had to remind him of home was a soft wool coat. Each spring his mother wove a new coat from the wool of her lambs and brought it to him.

Suddenly Samuel didn't feel important at all. He was just a priest's boy who hadn't even seen God's messengers. And he was lonely. He wanted to be at home with his parents instead of here in Shiloh. He sniffed the good smell of the pita again, and his eyes filled with tears.

"What's the matter, priest's boy? Are you sad?" The girl was tugging at his sash again. "Don't worry. Maybe you'll see God someday. Maybe even today."

He pulled away from her and ran to the sanctuary.

Eli the high priest was already waiting for Samuel. He stood at the top of the stone stairs that led from the sanctuary to the courtyard. Eli was a tall, thin man with a silver beard and pale, fogged-over eyes. The crowds of brightly dressed people waiting in the courtyard were only a blur of colors to him. He heard the hum of their voices and the bleating and lowing of the goats and bullocks they had brought as gifts to God. Then he heard Samuel's quick steps and felt the boy's warm hand clasp his stiff fingers.

"It's time for the prayer and sacrifice, my son," said Eli. "Come, lead me to the altar." He put his hand on Samuel's shoulder, and they began to walk down the steps.

The crowd grew quiet. Everybody watched them and waited. As they walked, Samuel pulled back his shoulders and smoothed his sash. I *am* important, he told himself. Eli needs me. I'm lucky to be a priest's boy and serve God, even if... even if I'd rather live in Ramah with my parents.

The smell of incense wafted from the tall burners in the courtyard. It mixed with the smoke of meat scorching on the altar and the hot, sweet smell of the blood of the sacrifices. Eli stood before the altar and cried loud prayers to God. He prayed for good crops and the birth of healthy babies to strengthen the tribes of Israel. And he praised and thanked God for the sun and rain and the many blessings God had given to the people.

Samuel waited close beside the high priest, ready to help if he grew tired. Eli's two plump sons and their helpers stood on each side of the altar. They were busy dividing the meat of the sacrifice into portions. A part was for the priests, a part for God, and a part for the families that had brought the sacrificial animals.

Standing there in the sunny courtyard with the breeze ruffling his hair and eager worshipers crowding close, Samuel felt almost happy again. We're all working together, he thought. The priests, the people, and me. We're trying to follow God's laws, and we're bringing sacrifices to please God. It's good. Maybe Eli will let me be a priest when I grow up.

Suddenly an angry shout burst through the sounds of the courtyard.

"You took too much!" You left nothing for God!"

The hum of talk stopped. Even Eli stopped praying. Everybody turned to see who could be shouting in this holy place. A thin man with bony elbows and knees poking through a patched wool robe stood facing Eli's younger son who was one of the priests. The priest was holding a great, dripping chunk of meat he had taken as his share.

"Don't be greedy. God will share the portion I left for your family," said the priest. His round belly shook as he laughed loudly. Then his eyes narrowed. "Move along," he shouted. "Who is next?"

"No!" The man refused to move. "You haven't left enough. After I give the required portion to God, there will be nothing left for my family."

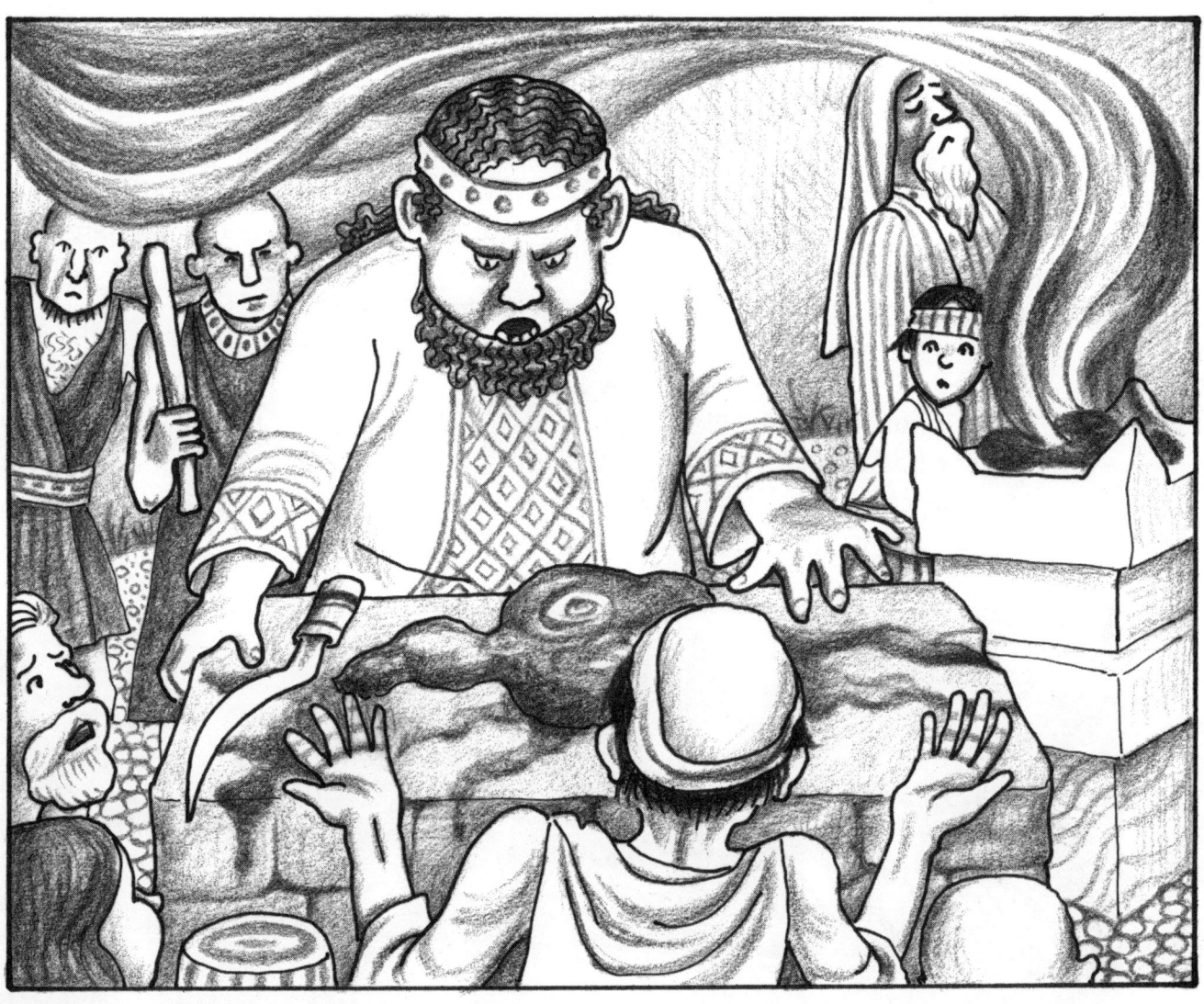

"That's your problem, not mine. Move!" the priest shouted again.

Two sanctuary guards stepped forward with clubs raised. The man shrank back from them and looked around for help. Nobody moved. He bowed his head and slowly walked away. Another worshiper took his place. Then the hum of talk and the chant of prayer rose again. Everything seemed as sunny and peaceful as before.

But Samuel clenched his fists. It's not fair, he thought. The poor man wasn't greedy. It was that pig, the son of Eli. How could he do that? How could Eli let him? Samuel looked up at the high priest. Eli must have heard what happened. Didn't he care that his son was robbing the people?

The old man stood stiff and straight, still singing the prayer of sacrifice. But his hand shook against Samuel's shoulder, and tears were rolling down his wrinkled cheeks and into his beard.

That night Samuel lay on his bed in the room next to the ancient ark. He was confused and sad. He pulled his new coat up to his chin and curled his cold legs in under it. The coat smelled of sun and hay. There was a lump in his throat. Why do I have to be here in Shiloh? he wondered. It's not a good place. Not for God and not for me. God wouldn't want to be served by thieves like Eli's sons. But they're the priests. They can do what they like.

He punched the pillow angrily. Well, I don't have to help them! I'm going home. That's what I'll do.

The coat hugged him. He thought of home and grew warmer and happier and sleepier. . . .

"SAMUEL." A deep voice rumbled through his dreams.

Samuel sprang up in bed. Eli was calling. He tiptoed through the hall with his toes cringing against the cold tile. He passed the sanctuary, where the ancient ark stood. A dim light burned in front of it throwing great, batlike shadows of the angels against the walls. He raced past and skidded into Eli's room. The high priest lay with his eyes closed and his white beard spread on his chest.

"Here I am," said Samuel. "You called me."

Eli's eyes blinked open. "I didn't call you," he said. "Go back to sleep."

Samuel ran back, jumped into his still-warm bed, and fell asleep.

"SAMUEL." The deep voice sounded in the darkness once more.

The boy shot up again. Shivering, he pulled the coat over his shoulders and padded through the dark hall to Eli's room. Again Eli was sleeping.

"Here I am," Samuel said, "because you called me."

Eli's eyes opened wide. His white brows drew together in puzzlement. "No, my son. I didn't call," he said. "Lie down again."

A third time Samuel was awakened by the powerful call in the night. "SAMUEL!"

He ran to Eli's room for the third time. And this time Eli understood. It was God who was calling Samuel. "Go and lie down," he said to the boy, "and if God calls again, you must say, 'Speak, God; your servant is listening.'"

"God?" Samuel's heart pounded, and his hair prickled as though it were standing straight up. As he hurried past the ark it seemed alive. The great angel shadows trembled on the wall. He crawled into bed, breathing hard, and waited.

"SAMUEL! SAMUEL!"

"S-speak, G-god; your servant is listening," Samuel gasped.

And God said to Samuel, "I will do a thing in Israel that will make the ears of every listener tingle. I will judge the house of Eli forever because he knew his sons were doing evil against Me, and he did not stop them. The sins of the house of Eli shall never be washed away. Not with sacrifices, not with offerings. Never!"

The small room grew quiet again. But God's words kept sounding in Samuel's ears as he lay awake.... "Never, never, the sins shall never be washed away...."

At last dawn shone gray at the windows, and Samuel got up to open the doors of the sanctuary. Eli heard and called to him, "Come here, my son, and tell me what God said to you."

Samuel told him the hard words of God.

The old priest listened, staring at the boy through milky-veiled eyes. Then he clasped his hands tightly together, and again the tears ran down his wrinkled cheeks. "Let God do what seems good in God's eyes," he said.

"What does God mean?" Samuel asked. "Without the house of Eli, who will be the priests? Who will speak to God for Israel? And who will speak to Israel for God?"

Eli didn't answer. Then, deep inside himself, Samuel felt the answer. It frightened him. But at the same time it warmed him like the soft, sweet-smelling coat his mother had made. I will become a priest. God will be with me and speak to me, he thought. God will tell me how to serve God and the people of Israel. And even though I won't go home, I won't be lonely anymore.

Here's what happened next. . . .

Things grew worse and worse for the tribes of Israel while Samuel was growing up in Shiloh. The enemy Philistines pressed into the heart of the country, captured the Holy Ark, and killed Eli's sons in a bloody battle. Eli died when he heard the tragic news, and Samuel became the new leader of his people. He united them in battle and judged them in peacetime, traveling from city to city. It was hard work. When he grew old and tired, he appointed his sons to be judges. But they were as dishonest as Eli's sons had been. The people were disgusted. "We want a king," they demanded. "We want to be like other nations." God warned them through Samuel of the suffering a king would cause them. But the people insisted on having a king. God chose a young man from the tribe of Benjamin to be the first king of Israel, with Samuel as the high priest.

Writings

Here is Samuel's warning to the people. Only a few years later this prophecy came true.

This will be the custom of the king who will rule you:
He will take your sons to drive his chariots and to be his horsemen,
And some will run before his chariot.
He will appoint captains over thousands and captains over fifties
And set them to plow his ground, reap his harvest, and make his weapons.
And he will take your daughters for perfumers, cooks, and bakers,
And he will take your fields, vineyards, and olive groves and give them to his servants...
...And you will cry out on that day because of the king that you have chosen.
And God will not hear you on that day.

Based on I Samuel 8:11-14, 18

SAMUEL'S SCRAMBLED WORDS

C _ _ _ _ _ _ _
TOCHAIR

P _ _ _ _ _ _
TREPIS

A _ _ _
LAATR

C _ _ _ _ _ _ _ _ _ _ _
MADSCTNNOMME

P _ _ _ _ _ _ _ _ _
TIHNPILISE

Check your answers on page 80.

35

CHOOSE!

If you were Samuel, where would you choose to be?
— at Little League
— at school
— tending to the sheep
— serving God and Eli at Shiloh
— helping out at home

Did you choose the space next to the bottom? If you didn't, you are thinking like many of the prophets. They did not want to be prophets. They knew God would tell them to criticize the Jewish people and to predict terrible punishment. People would hate them for bringing such bad news. But when God called on the prophets to serve, they obeyed–whether they liked it or not.

There may be times when you have to do things that are important and right–but they scare or bore you, or you just don't want to do them. Think of three such things.

1.

2.

3.

Do you end up doing what you have to do?
☐ yes

☐ no

How do you feel about it?

LONG LIVE KING "WHAT'S HIS NAME."

When the people demanded a king, God chose a young shepherd for the job. Here's a rebus that tells you the name of the first king of Israel.
Check your answer on page 80.

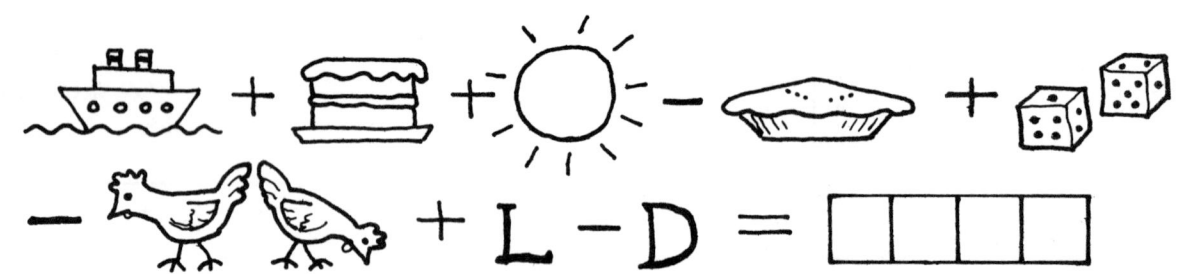

36

ELIJAH

4.

After Saul two more kings ruled over the Land of Israel. They were David and Solomon. David was a fighter who led Israel in many wars to protect its borders. Solomon was a wise, learned man who wrote beautiful poetry. He also loved to build fancy palaces, new fortress cities, and a great, powerful army. Solomon built the gleaming marble Temple in Jerusalem to hold the ancient Ark of the Covenant. To pay for his army, his buildings, and his thousand wives, Solomon squeezed heavy taxes from his people. When he died, his son, the new king, demanded even more money. The people of the northern part of the kingdom refused to pay. They broke away and formed a new kingdom called Israel. The southern part, which stayed loyal to Solomon's son, was called Judah. Israel, in the north, was influenced by the customs and religions of other peoples. A prophet called Elijah was sent by God to warn Ahab, king of Israel, to obey the Torah. Ahab's wife, Queen Jezebel, got very angry at the interference and decided to silence Elijah forever.

More of the story...

MURDERER IN THE VINEYARD

He was so tired of running, running and hiding like a hunted animal. Elijah peered out between the spiky branches of a broom tree and listened. He heard the hot afternoon wind howling over the bare hills, but there was no sound of his enemies. Queen Jezebel's soldiers must have given up the search. For a while he was safe.

Elijah stretched his stiff legs, leaned his shaggy head against the tree trunk, and tried to rest. But he was too unhappy to fall asleep. "God, O God, take my life!" he cried, staring up into the bright, harsh sky. "I've failed! I can't bring Your words to the Israelites. They tore down Your altars and killed Your prophets. I'm the only one left, and I'm so lonely. Let me die, too."

Only a few days before he had been so happy. He had won a great victory over four-hundred-and-fifty priests of the false god Baal. On that day King Ahab, the Israelites, the priests, and Elijah had climbed to the top of Mount Carmel. There the priests of Baal had labored to light a fire on the altar of their god. They had failed. Then Elijah had called to God for help, and the fire on God's altar had blazed up immediately.

37

The excited, triumphant prophet had called on the people to kill all of the four-hundred-and-fifty false prophets.

It was a great success for God and for Elijah, but it turned Jezebel the queen purple with rage! She sent her soldiers out to track Elijah down and kill him.

Now the prophet lay alone in the desert watching the sky darken and thinking, It's a hopeless fight. I've had enough. God, please, please let me die.

But God was not finished with Elijah. In a still, small voice God spoke and told Elijah he must go on. God was not ready to give up hope for the people of Israel. There were still Israelites who would hear Elijah's message. He must keep trying.

Elijah was not the only unhappy man in the land. In the great ivory palace in Samaria, King Ahab was stamping around, wearing out a track in the soft sheepskin rugs. He was frightened, angry, and greedily jealous, all at the same time.

Jezebel leaned back on the couch twirling her jeweled necklace and watching him. Finally he stopped, turned to her, and waved his arms with exasperation, so that all his bracelets tinkled and jingled. "You didn't have to drive Elijah off and try to kill him!" he shouted. "After all, he *is* a prophet. He speaks for God!"

"He's a miserable, skinny, hairy, little man, and he speaks for only one god–the god of the Hebrews," Jezebel said frostily. "Where did he get the nerve to stand up against my priests? And what right did he have to order the people to kill the priests of Baal?" Her voice grew louder. "That was too much! My priests were fools because they failed miserably on Mount Carmel, so maybe *I* should have killed them. But Elijah had no right–"

"Of course he had a right," Ahab interrupted her. "He's an Israelite prophet, and he is speaking for the God of Israel, and I am the king of Israel, and don't you forget it!" His face turned red as a tomato, and he stopped to take a breath, which gave Jezebel a chance to jump up and poke her finger at his nose while she yelled, "You may be the king, but I am a princess of Sidon and the queen of this country! That wild man dressed in animal skins has no right to burst into my kingdom and order me around!"

They glared at each other, trying to stare each other down. Then Jezebel's black-rimmed eyes crinkled into a smile, and she reached out and patted the king's cheek. "Darling, why should we fight?" she said in a velvety voice. "We don't have to argue about Elijah anymore. He's gone. Now we can pray and bring sacrifices to any god we want." She clapped her hands. "I have an idea. Why don't you pick out a nice, fat calf and bring it to your priests to sacrifice. If the God of Israel is upset with you, this will fix it. The smoke of a fat sacrifice will please even the fussiest god."

Ahab plopped down onto the couch, shook his head, and stared gloomily out the window.

"Now what are you pouting about?" she asked.

"Things aren't as simple for me as they are for you," he complained. "I still have some rules to follow."

"Don't be silly. Kings and queens make their own rules." She leaned over and kissed the bald spot on the top of his head. "Just tell me, darling, what you want."

"Nothing. Nothing you can help me with," he mumbled.

"Tell me, lovey, please. What do you want?"

"That." Ahab pointed out the window, past the flowers and vines of his own garden and on beyond the stone fence to the next vineyard where vines looped over trellises and great clusters of grapes hung down.

"What? That vineyard?" she asked.

He nodded. "It's Naboth's vineyard. And it's a perfect place for a palace vegetable garden, so close that I could have fresh onions and cucumbers for breakfast every day."

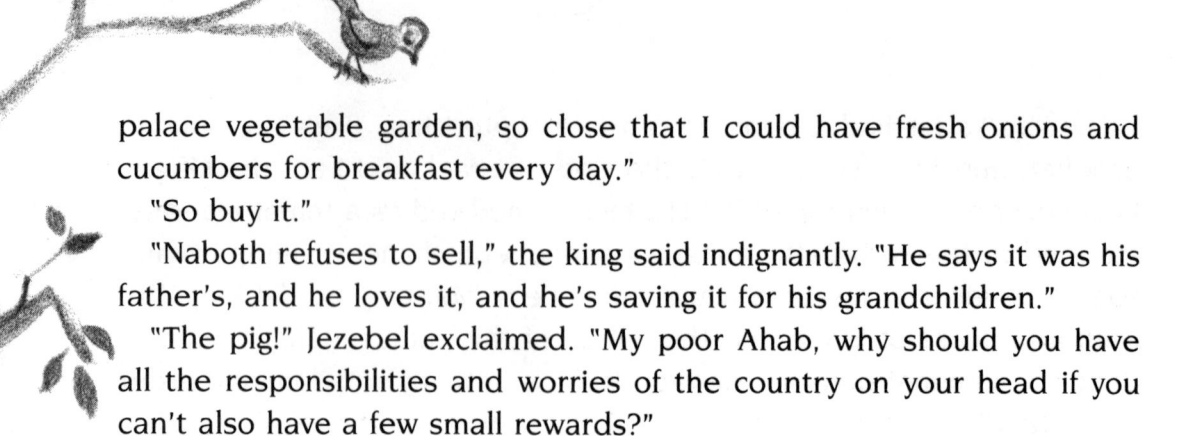

"So buy it."

"Naboth refuses to sell," the king said indignantly. "He says it was his father's, and he loves it, and he's saving it for his grandchildren."

"The pig!" Jezebel exclaimed. "My poor Ahab, why should you have all the responsibilities and worries of the country on your head if you can't also have a few small rewards?"

He sniffed in sad, suffering agreement.

"Don't you worry about a thing. I'll take care of it," Jezebel said. "If my sweet king wants Naboth's vineyard, he shall have it."

"Yes, well . . . listen, don't break any laws," Ahab protested feebly. But Jezebel had already swished out the door. Ahab settled onto the couch, leaned back, and closed his eyes. But instead of dreaming about Naboth's lush vineyard or a fresh cucumber-onion breakfast, he found himself thinking uneasily, I wonder what Elijah is doing. I hope he isn't too angry at me.

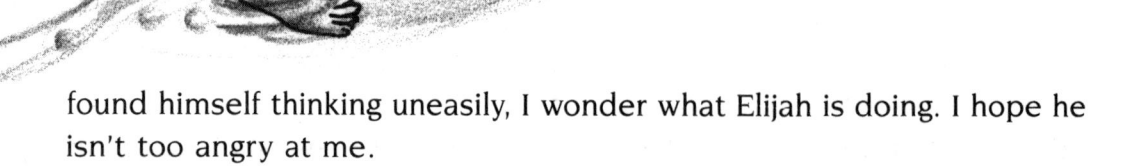

Just as Ahab was worrying about Elijah, the prophet was thinking about Ahab. Elijah had walked a long way since escaping from Jezebel. And walking helped him to think. Now he sat soaking his feet in a brook and making plans. King Ahab isn't all bad, he thought. I know I can reach him with God's message to destroy the temples of Baal and to follow God's law. But maybe I've been too rough. Maybe I have to explain and persuade instead of yelling and threatening. He examined a blister, wiggled his toes in the lukewarm water, and sighed contentedly. He felt better now. He'd go back to Ahab and try being nice.

But Elijah never had a chance to try. On the way back to Israel, Elijah heard the terrible news of what had happened to Naboth and his vineyard. Jezebel had paid two men to report to the judges of the city that Naboth had cursed God and the king right in front of them. Though Naboth cried and protested, "No, I didn't, I didn't! It's a lie!" he was dragged out of his house, taken to the place of execution, and stoned to death. Now the green, fruit-filled vineyard belonged to the king.

The fury of God filled Elijah. Ahab was a murderer! He could never use explanations or persuasion with a murderer. He had to find the king, accuse him of murder, and tell him of the terrible punishment God would impose on him. With fists clenched and anger in his heart Elijah continued on the road to Samaria–to Ahab and Jezebel's ivory palace.

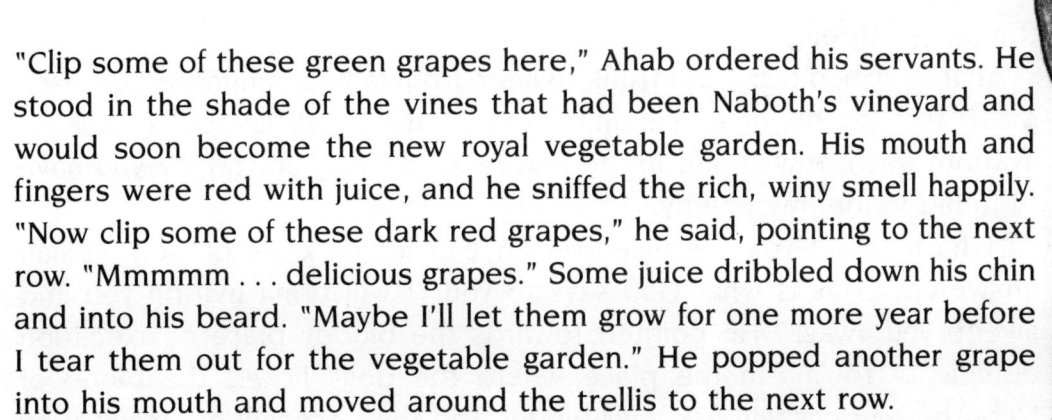

"Clip some of these green grapes here," Ahab ordered his servants. He stood in the shade of the vines that had been Naboth's vineyard and would soon become the new royal vegetable garden. His mouth and fingers were red with juice, and he sniffed the rich, winy smell happily. "Now clip some of these dark red grapes," he said, pointing to the next row. "Mmmmm . . . delicious grapes." Some juice dribbled down his chin and into his beard. "Maybe I'll let them grow for one more year before I tear them out for the vegetable garden." He popped another grape into his mouth and moved around the trellis to the next row.

"Now let's take these maroon ones," he began . . . but the words shriveled in his mouth when he saw a dark, lean figure waiting among the lush vines. Elijah was leathery-brown from the desert sun, and his head was a tangle of wiry hair and beard, like a lion's mane. A dry desert wind seemed to swirl around him and curl the leaves nearby. Ahab tottered backward as Elijah raised a long, bony arm.

"Have you murdered and then become the inheritor?" Elijah's voice thundered through the vineyard.

Ahab grabbed a gnarled trunk to keep from falling. A hundred excuses raced through his head—I didn't know.... It was all Jezebel's idea.... Naboth was a traitor—but in the end he could only stutter, "Y-you have f-f-found m-me, my enemy."

"I have found you because you do evil in the eyes of God," Elijah answered. "This is what God says to you: 'I will bring evil on you and sweep you away!'" He pointed towards the bloody place of execution outside of town. "In the place where the dogs licked the blood of Naboth, the dogs will lick your blood. And the dogs will eat Jezebel by the walls of Yizreel!"

His burning eyes seemed to scorch the trembling king for a long moment, then Elijah turned and left the vineyard. Ahab leaned against the stolen vines, gulping great sobs. Slowly he slipped to the ground and began to rip at his fine, royal robes. "I've sinned. I did wrong. I'm sorry," he cried over and over.

When Jezebel found Ahab, he was sitting on the ground between the vines, wearing tattered robes and rocking back and forth while he fasted.

"Darling, you must eat something," she said anxiously. "Why are you punishing yourself?"

He shook his head. "I've sinned," he groaned.

"What did you do that was so terrible? You're the king! Be brave. Catch the big-mouthed prophet and throw him in jail. Cut out his tongue!"

"No. The prophet spoke the truth. I disobeyed God's law. And God is a greater king than I am." Ahab started to sob again.

"I give up!" Jezebel shouted. "I'll never understand you Israelites. You are your own worst enemies. You're always making yourselves miserable."

If Elijah had heard her as he trudged back to the desert, he might have smiled a sour smile and said, "When we Israelites don't do God's bidding, we are miserable. But sometimes even when we do God's bidding, it makes us miserable."

Writings

Elisha was a student of the prophet Elijah. He followed him and would not leave him even when Elijah was about to die.

> Elijah said to him, "Remain here, I beg you, because God has sent me to the Jordan River." And Elisha said, "I will not leave you." They walked on and stood by the Jordan. Elijah took off his mantle, rolled it up, and struck the water. It was divided to one side and to the other so that they walked across on dry ground. When they had crossed over, Elijah asked, "What shall I do for you before I am taken away?" And Elisha answered, "Let a double portion of your spirit be upon me...."
> As they went on and talked, a chariot of fire and horses of fire appeared. The chariot and horses came between the two men, and Elijah was swept up into the heavens by a storm wind. Elisha cried, "My father, my father—(I see) the chariots of Israel and their horsemen!" And he did not see Elijah again.

Based on II Kings 2:6-12

In later years people believed that Elijah had not died—he had only been taken up to heaven. Stories were told about how this stern prophet came down to earth in disguise and helped people who were in trouble. Even now we put a glass of wine on the seder table at Passover for the most honored guest—Elijah the prophet. And we open the door to invite him to join us. The happiest belief about Elijah is that he will come down from heaven to announce the news that the Messiah is coming, bringing with him a happier, more peaceful world.

PUPPET POWWOW

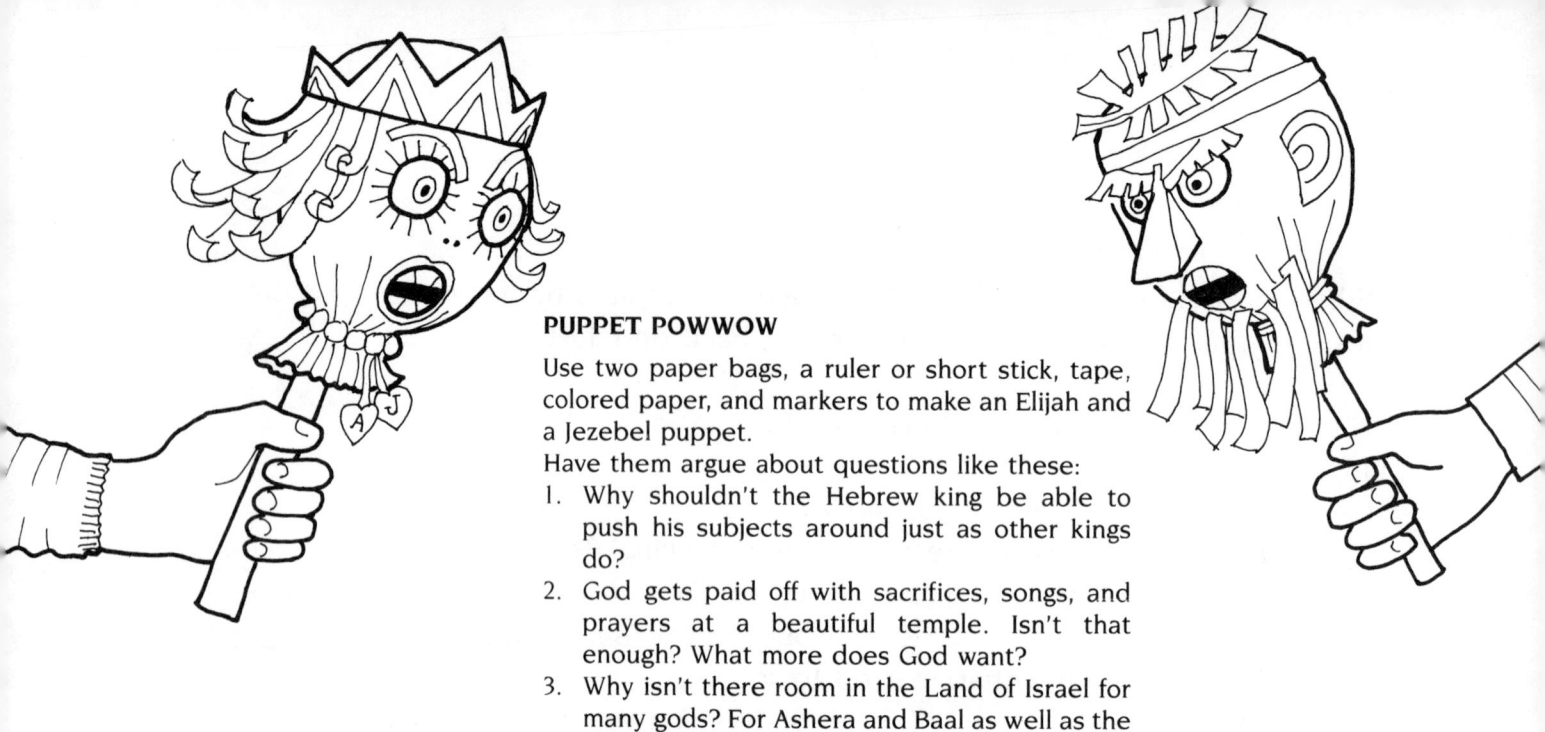

Use two paper bags, a ruler or short stick, tape, colored paper, and markers to make an Elijah and a Jezebel puppet.
Have them argue about questions like these:
1. Why shouldn't the Hebrew king be able to push his subjects around just as other kings do?
2. God gets paid off with sacrifices, songs, and prayers at a beautiful temple. Isn't that enough? What more does God want?
3. Why isn't there room in the Land of Israel for many gods? For Ashera and Baal as well as the Hebrew God?
4. Why does Elijah keep picking on Jezebel–and vice versa?

ELIJAH STORIES

In the Bible Elijah is a sad, fierce man. But in later stories he is warm and helpful. He comes to earth as a peasant or a peddler and helps needy people. Here is the story of Elijah and a poor family. Can you fill in the captions?

Can you write a modern Elijah story? Use this space to tell how Elijah might sweep out of the heavens like a prophet-superman and solve an impossible problem. Add another page if you write a long story.

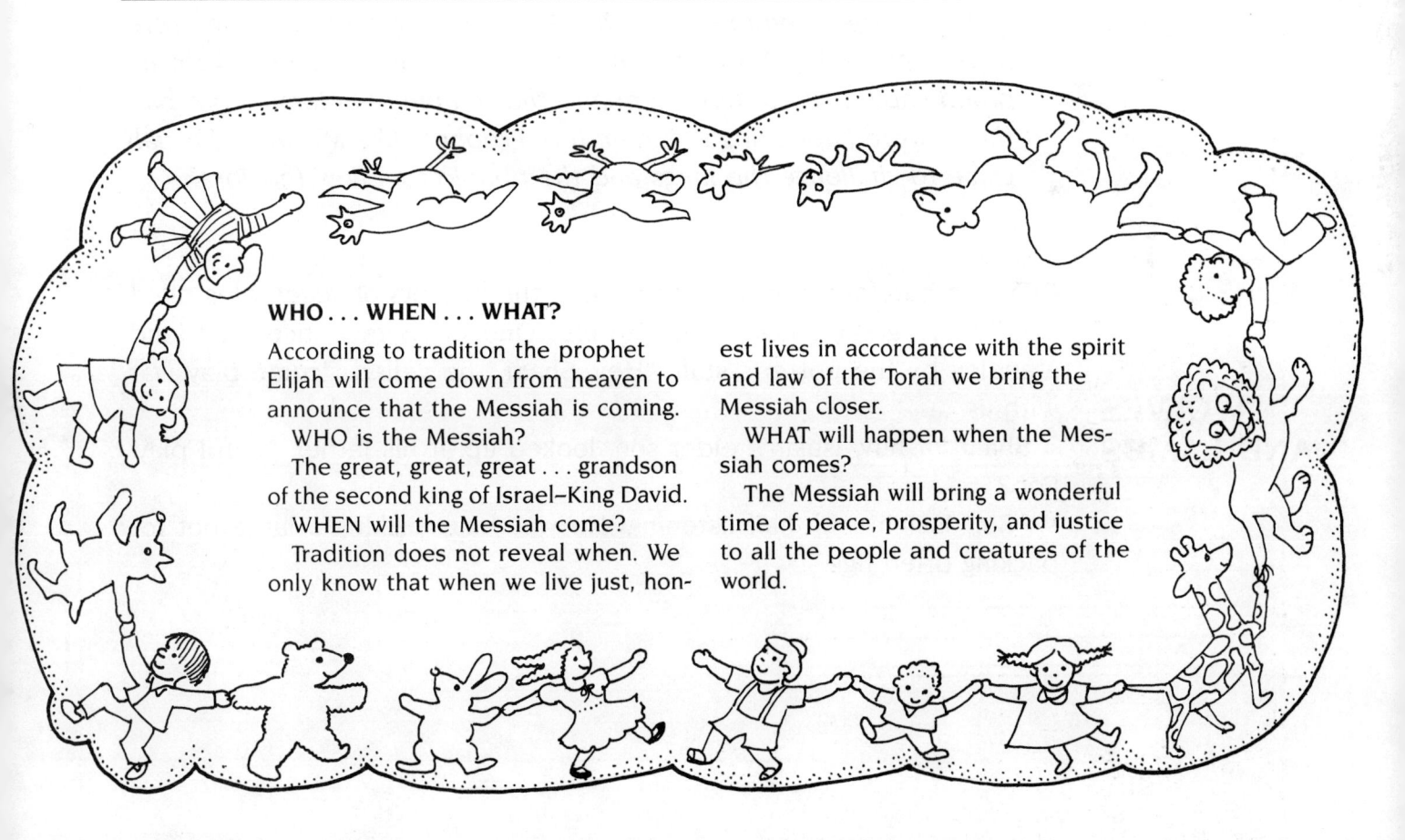

_____
_____
_____
_____
_____
_____
_____
_____
_____
_____
_____
_____

WHO... WHEN... WHAT?

According to tradition the prophet Elijah will come down from heaven to announce that the Messiah is coming.

WHO is the Messiah?

The great, great, great... grandson of the second king of Israel–King David.

WHEN will the Messiah come?

Tradition does not reveal when. We only know that when we live just, honest lives in accordance with the spirit and law of the Torah we bring the Messiah closer.

WHAT will happen when the Messiah comes?

The Messiah will bring a wonderful time of peace, prosperity, and justice to all the people and creatures of the world.

5. ISAIAH

The story goes on....

About seventy years after the time of Elijah the prophet Amos left his work of herding cattle and came to Israel to bring a new message. He warned the people and the king that it was not as important to bring gifts and sacrifices to God as it was to behave kindly and honestly toward one another.

> I despise your feasts, and I will not smell the sacrifices of your solemn assemblies. Though you offer Me burnt offerings and meal offerings I will not accept them.... But let justice roll down like waters and righteousness like a mighty stream.
>
> Amos 5:21-24

After Amos had frightened people almost to death with terrible threats of punishment and exile from their land because of their misdeeds, he finished his prophecy with these hopeful words:

> "I will bring back My captive people of Israel, and they shall rebuild the ruined cities and inhabit them.... I will plant them upon their land, and they shall no more be plucked up out of their land," says the Lord your God.
>
> Amos 9:14-15

The sad predictions Amos had made came true. The northern realm of Israel was conquered by the Assyrians, and the people were driven into exile. Now only the realm of Judah remained, with its proud capital city of Jerusalem and the Temple of Solomon. But bad things were happening in Judah, too. Prophets like Micah and Isaiah came to challenge the kings and the people to follow the Torah.

WOLVES AND LAMBS

Three barefoot boys raced between the baskets of vegetables piled by the great gate of the Temple. One of them noticed a friend standing by the potter's stall. "Hey, Shaar," he yelled, "come play war with us."

Shaar Yashuv, Isaiah's elder son, looked up at his father. "Can I play, Pop?"

"Go," Isaiah said, half listening. He was busy picking a large pot for packing dried figs.

"You be the Assyrians, the bad guys," said the biggest boy, pointing to Shaar and a smaller boy. "Me and Moshe will be the Judeans."

"No, *you* be the bad guys," Shaar Yashuv shouted. "This old cart is our fortress. You can't come in here."

"Yeah, stay out, you dirty Assyrians!" yelled his friend.

Pebbles showered the cart. The boys ducked, but a rock hit Shaar Yashuv on the forehead. "Ow, that hurt. It's not fair to use such big rocks!" he cried. "I'm telling my father." He ran back to the potter's stall.

"Tch, tch, tch..." Isaiah clucked sympathetically, feeling his son's head. "You'll have a bump, but you're all right. But I don't want you to throw rocks. Next time you might really get hurt, or hurt your friend."

"No, I won't," Shaar said. "We're just playing make-believe war."

"Playing war is an evil, dangerous game," Isaiah said firmly. "Stop it!"

The potter looked up from his wheel. "What's so evil about it? It's life. Let the kids play. Soon enough they'll grow up and have to fight a serious war against the Assyrians."

"Do you know what you're saying?" Isaiah's eyes opened wide, and his brown beard bristled. He shoved the pot aside and banged the potter's table. "A serious war against the Assyrians will destroy Jerusalem. God has sent Assyria to punish Judah for its evil ways. How can Judah win a war against God's messenger?"

Shaar Yashuv circled his father uneasily. "Pa,"–he tugged at his robe–" Mama said to bring the pot home quickly. She has to pack the figs." But he knew it was useless to ask. When his father took off on one of his speeches, he couldn't hear anything else.

Shaar Yashuv knew his father was different from other people. Part of him was an ordinary father who bought jars for figs and fixed bruises. But the other part was special and scary. Shaar Yashuv could always tell when the other part was going to surface because Isaiah's eyes would widen, his face would get red, and his hair and beard would bristle... like right now. At such times he wasn't Isaiah the father, he was Isaiah the prophet, who spoke to God and who spoke the words of God in a strange, ringing voice.

47

Isaiah's voice was ringing out now, saying, "God will not help Judah in a war. God does not want military victories. God wants Judah to do right, to care for the orphans and the widows, to have fair courts and honest judges...."

The bustle of trading stopped as people turned and listened to the stocky, dignified, white-robed man. Two noblewomen shopping at a perfume stall looked up scornfully. One of them pointed a plump arm loaded with gold bracelets at Isaiah. "That one is a troublemaker," she said loudly.

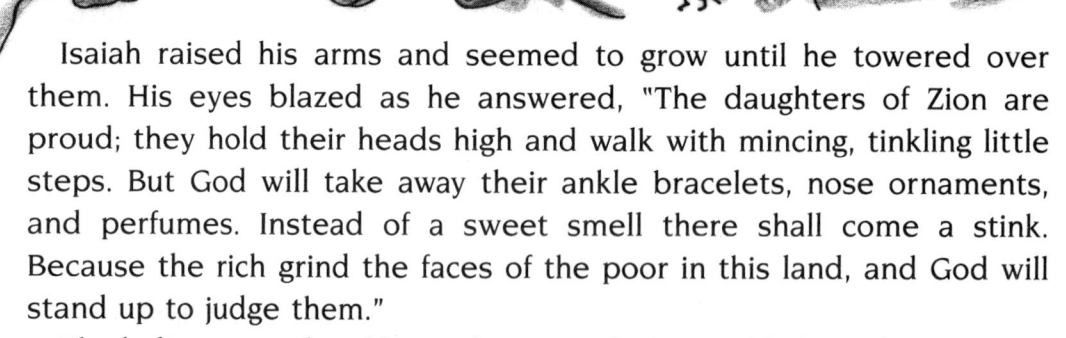

Isaiah raised his arms and seemed to grow until he towered over them. His eyes blazed as he answered, "The daughters of Zion are proud; they hold their heads high and walk with mincing, tinkling little steps. But God will take away their ankle bracelets, nose ornaments, and perfumes. Instead of a sweet smell there shall come a stink. Because the rich grind the faces of the poor in this land, and God will stand up to judge them."

The ladies gasped and hurried away with their ankle bracelets tinkling, but the crowd stood and listened.

On the rooftop of the Temple storehouse near the gate, two of the most powerful men in Judah were also listening to Isaiah. One had a rosy, clear-eyed face and a mass of curly hair under a gold headband. He was the new young king of Judah, Hezekiah. The other, elegantly dressed in a jewel-encrusted robe, was the king's wily adviser Sabua.

"Tell me, prophet," called King Hezekiah, "why is God angry? We make fat sacrifices each day at the Temple. Priests and Levites recite prayers and sing praises to God. What more can we do?"

"Come and walk with me in the city. I'll show you why God is angry," Isaiah challenged him.

"Don't do it, Your Majesty. This man doesn't speak for God. He's a crank," Sabua said sharply as Hezekiah stood up. "Besides, it's . . . it's unhealthy for Your Majesty to walk in the hot sun."

"But it's cool and cloudy." Hezekiah laughed over his shoulder as he ran down the steps. His guards clattered after him, and Sabua scurried close behind, his face tight and fists clenched with anger.

At the gate Shaar tugged at his father's robe again. "Pa, Mama said–"

"Take the pot home, and leave me be. I'm busy!" Isaiah roared.

"All right, all right." Shaar backed off. He trudged back to the potter complaining, "Now Mama is going to get mad at *me*; I know she will!"

Walking quickly, Isaiah led the king and his party down from the Temple Mount into the city. They passed the high walls of the king's palace and the gate of Sabua's mansion. People sat in the dust and lay against the walls of the buildings, wrapped in wool robes and goatskins to keep out the dampness. A crying child raised his hands to them.

"These are homeless people, refugees from Samaria," Isaiah said. "They are suffering because King Hoshea of Samaria disobeyed God and led his country into war against Assyria. The Assyrians defeated Hoshea, destroyed Israel, and dragged the people off to exile. Only a few escaped to Judah."

"It was a just war!" Sabua cried indignantly. "The Assyrians were squeezing every shekel out of Samaria. King Hoshea had to fight!"

"The Assyrians were God's tool to punish Samaria. If the people of Samaria had worshiped God and treated one another justly, they would not have had to fight," Isaiah answered.

Hezekiah said nothing. He just listened and looked with wide, thoughtful eyes.

The ground sloped down ahead of them. They saw smoke rising behind a line of trees. Isaiah led them down winding steps into the Valley of Hinnom. Great stone altars to the gods Moloch and Ashera stood here with tall trees shading them. They heard the clashing of cymbals and beating of drums as musicians and worshipers crowded around the altars. Frightened, wild-eyed animals bawled in pens, waiting to be sacrificed, while the fatty black smoke of earlier sacrifices billowed up from the altars.

The worshipers bowed to the young king. He smiled and nodded, but his smile froze as Isaiah spoke again.

"Today there are only sheep and goats in the pens. There are no little boys and girls. Last month three children had their throats cut and were thrown into the flaming belly of the god Moloch," he said.

Hezekiah shivered. "Is this true?" he asked Sabua. "Have children been sacrificed here?"

Sabua hesitated, but Isaiah answered for him, "Your own half-brother, the son of your father, King Ahaz, was sacrificed to Moloch."

"It was politics, Your Majesty," Sabua cried. "King Ahaz had to show our Phoenician allies that he respected their god, Moloch. It was a noble, patriotic gesture of friendship."

"It was murder!" Isaiah rasped. "Even worse–it was the worship of false gods. How can men and women bow down to the work of their own hands, to idols their own fingers have made, and forget the God of their parents?"

"That's a very narrow-minded, old-fashioned opinion!" Sabua was outraged. "King Hezekiah is a modern monarch and understands–"

"Be quiet," snapped Hezekiah. "Lead on, Isaiah."

Back up the steps and through the city they went. It was beginning to drizzle. The king's guards forced their way past hurrying litters and chariots carrying well-fed, jeweled, and powdered Jerusalemites. They whipped aside peasants and slaves carrying heavy loads.

"The rich trample the poor in Jerusalem," Isaiah exclaimed. "Once this city was full of justice, but now it is the home of murderers. To seek fair judgment, help the oppressed, plead for the widow–this is what God wants of us."

"Not true!" sputtered Sabua. "Rich people don't trample on purpose. They get rich because they're smart at business or because they own good farm land. They deserve every shekel they own, as long as they pay their taxes to the king and the Temple and bring the proper sacrifices."

They had reached the palace, and the drizzle was turning to rain. Hezekiah mopped his face. "Thank you, gentlemen. I've seen enough," he said. "My feet hurt, and my robe is soaked. I'm going to take a hot bath and think about what you've both said. Good day."

Shaar was busy packing figs into the new pot and eating a few on the side when he saw his father hurrying home through the rain. He looks normal, thought Shaar. I can talk to him.

"Hi, Pop." He squeezed the words out through a mouthful of figs as his father came in the doorway. He helped him pull off the wet robe. "Mama was really mad that I got home so late. She was mad at you, too, till I told her you were with the king. How did you do?"

"I don't know," Isaiah answered, and sank wearily down on the mat.

The answer to Shaar Yashuv's question came a few weeks before Passover. In a decree that shook the land of Judah, King Hezekiah ordered the altars in the Hinnom Valley to be torn down. The hilltop shrines all through Judah where the people worshiped many gods were to be destroyed. The Temple was to be cleaned and purified, and all the people of Judah would come to Jerusalem for a great celebration and a Passover feast at the house of God. The final important decision was about Sabua. He had been dismissed from his job as royal adviser.

Isaiah glowed with joy as he and Shaar Yashuv stood at the top of the steps leading to the Hinnom Valley and watched the stone altars come crashing down. Brown dust rose into the air and made the boy sneeze.

He blew his nose and asked, "How about the other important stuff, like helping poor people and keeping peace with the Assyrians?"

"I'm working on it." Isaiah sighed. "God won't let me stop. I'm sure a time will come when people will want to help one another and live together in peace." Then his eyes widened, his hair and beard began to bristle, and his voice grew deeper and stronger. Uh-oh, thought Shaar Yashuv with a shiver, this is Pa's prophet voice. He's not just talking to me. He's talking to all of Judah. Maybe even to the whole world.

"The time will come when men and women will learn to live peacefully," said Isaiah, "and the wolf shall dwell with the lamb, and the leopard shall lie down with the kid, and the calf and the young lion shall graze together. And a little child shall lead them. And the cow and the bear shall feed; their young ones shall lie down together. And the lion shall eat straw like the ox.... They shall not hurt nor destroy in all My holy mountain. For the earth shall be full of the knowledge of God as the waters cover the sea." (Isaiah 11:6-9)

"Amen," breathed Shaar Yashuv, feeling very proud and hopeful but a little afraid of the prophet-father who stood beside him.

Writings

Isaiah warned, scolded, and lectured the people of Judah. But he also had some happy things to say. He promised that one day ancient enemies would learn to live together as friends:

> In that day there shall be a highway from Egypt to Assyria and (the people of) Assyria will come to Egypt and (those of) Egypt will come to Assyria and they shall worship together. In that day Israel as well as Egypt and Assyria will be a blessing in the land. The Lord will bless them, saying, "Blessed be Egypt My people, and Assyria My handiwork, and Israel–My inheritance."
>
> Isaiah 19:23-25

> Out of Zion shall go forth Torah and the word of the Lord from Jerusalem. The Lord shall judge among the nations.... And they shall beat their swords into plowshares and their spears into pruning hooks. Nation shall not lift up sword against nation, nor shall they learn war anymore.
>
> Isaiah 2:3-4

CHANGING

Both Amos and Isaiah warned that sacrifices and ceremonies were not as important as behaving justly toward one another. They called upon the Israelites and the king to become better people.

Can people change?

Have you changed?

Fold a paper into four parts. Write a milestone or turning point of your life on three sections–for example, starting kindergarten, first trip to summer camp, birth of a sister or brother.

Write on each of the three sections the ways that you changed and the ways you stayed the same.

Write on the fourth section things you like about yourself today and things you'd like to change.

Age 3 my kid sister was born	Age 5 I started Kindergarten
Age 9 I went to summer camp	things I like about myself things I want to change

Isaiah's prophecy of turning "swords into plowshares" is carved into a courtyard wall at the United Nations in New York.

THE VINEYARD

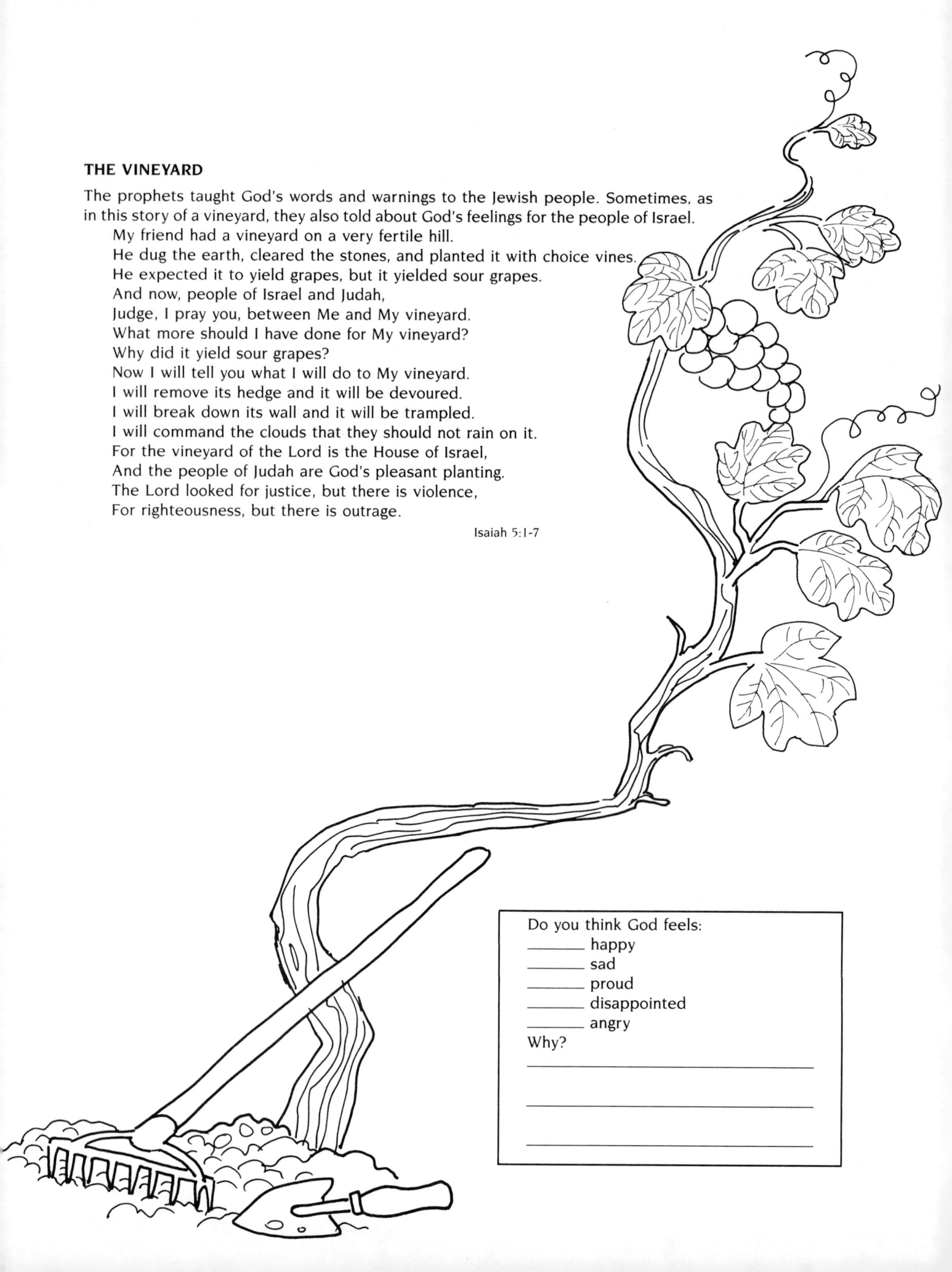

The prophets taught God's words and warnings to the Jewish people. Sometimes, as in this story of a vineyard, they also told about God's feelings for the people of Israel.

My friend had a vineyard on a very fertile hill.
He dug the earth, cleared the stones, and planted it with choice vines.
He expected it to yield grapes, but it yielded sour grapes.
And now, people of Israel and Judah,
Judge, I pray you, between Me and My vineyard.
What more should I have done for My vineyard?
Why did it yield sour grapes?
Now I will tell you what I will do to My vineyard.
I will remove its hedge and it will be devoured.
I will break down its wall and it will be trampled.
I will command the clouds that they should not rain on it.
For the vineyard of the Lord is the House of Israel,
And the people of Judah are God's pleasant planting.
The Lord looked for justice, but there is violence,
For righteousness, but there is outrage.

Isaiah 5:1-7

Do you think God feels:
_____ happy
_____ sad
_____ proud
_____ disappointed
_____ angry
Why?
_____
_____
_____

JEREMIAH

6.

Good kings and bad kings followed one another in the realm of Judah for the next hundred years. The smoke of sacrifices to God billowed up from the Temple altar every day, but the Torah laws that protected the poor and powerless were ignored. The kings of Judah got itchy for adventure and made treaties with their neighbors to go to war against common enemies. "Don't fight!" cried the prophets. "Trust in God, not in your armies or your allies!" In the middle of a disastrous war with Babylonia, the prophet Jeremiah risked his life to bring God's message to Judah.

The story goes on....

Jerusalem was as quiet as death. The archers who were defending the city from high atop the city wall were slumped against the shooting slots. Children sat in the dust playing listless games with pebbles. Only the space by the Temple gate was busy. Hungry people gathered there to trade for bits of bread and a few dry vegetables.

Jeremiah patted a little girl's curly hair as he walked toward the Temple. She smiled up at him, and he felt suddenly lonely. If only he could have had children. If only God hadn't commanded him to be alone, to be only a prophet. But it was just as well, he thought. If he had a child, he'd have to watch it slowly starve. Almost everybody in Jerusalem was starving.

Outside the city walls the bright tents of the enemy Babylonians billowed in the hot summer breeze. The smell of meat broiling over Babylonian campfires drifted up and tickled the noses of hungry Judean soldiers on the wall. The enemy had surrounded the city for weeks, not allowing food or other supplies to be brought in. They were in no hurry. Instead of fighting to capture Jerusalem they were starving the city to death.

"I'll trade this fine linen robe for a loaf of bread!"

"I offer a slice of bread. Take it or leave it!"

"Two carrots for a gold bracelet."

"A jug of red wine–what am I offered?"

"A sharp Tyrian dagger for the wine."

Jeremiah walked faster as he heard the traders at the gate. He pushed past little piles of goods. A lean woman looked up and saw the tall, gray-bearded prophet with bright, sad eyes. She poked her neighbor. "There goes the moaner-groaner," she snickered.

WHICH SIDE ARE YOU ON?

He heard and winced. Why do I keep trying to talk to them? he asked himself. They hate me. And sometimes I hate them, too. But he forced himself to move on into the crowd. He couldn't help it. The words of God were burning inside him. He had to speak.

In the center he stopped, braced his legs, and took a deep breath. Then he shouted above the sound of the haggling, "People of Judea, why are you fighting this war? You can't win. God has sent the Babylonians to capture Jerusalem and to punish you. You have forgotten God's laws. You cheat one another and steal from helpless people."

"Be quiet! You're a liar!" a man shouted from the Temple yard.

"God loves us. We're the Chosen People. God won't let us lose the war," a woman cried.

A boy yelled "Traitor!" and kicked a shower of pebbles at Jeremiah.

"Listen to me," Jeremiah pleaded, raising his arms. "Stop this useless war. There is still time. You can save yourselves and live in peace. End the war, go home, tend your farms in peace, and obey God."

More stones flew. Jeremiah shut his eyes and tried to shield his face, but he kept pleading, "God asks that you deal honestly with one another, observe the Sabbath, forget false gods."

There was a sudden clatter of armor and the thud of feet. The stones stopped flying. People shrank back as a group of the soldiers of Zedekiah, king of Jerusalem and Judea, burst through the crowd, surrounded Jeremiah, and dragged him through the gate into the Temple courtyard.

"Stop! Let me speak!" he protested as he was pulled through another gate, bumped over hot cobblestones, and then raised into the air.

"Drop him into the pit. Captain's orders," a gruff voice commanded.

"But he'll die down there. He's a prophet of God!"

"Says who? The captain says he's a traitor, ruining the fighting spirit of the army with his cowardly peace talk. Drop him!"

The bright sun disappeared, and Jeremiah felt himself falling, clutching and scratching against rough stone walls, falling. With a wrenching thud he hit the bottom of the pit. And as he lay stunned, slimy, cold mud began to suck at his body. Jeremiah struggled to his feet. The mud reached to his knees and was pulling at his thighs. He looked up. High above was a circle of light. "Pull me out!" he cried. His voice bounced against the oozing rocks. Nobody looked down. Nobody answered.

He was shivering, and his teeth were chattering. He leaned his aching body against the wall. Is this how my life will end, God? he thought. All these years You've forced me to teach the people Your Torah. I didn't want the job–You forced me. And now, when they face death, You take me away. Who will show them how to save themselves if I die here in this pit?

The mud oozed through his clothing, and the cold crept into his flesh and bones. He stopped hoping. There was no future for his people. He would die. The Judeans would be killed or dragged into captivity. God's Chosen People would disappear. Jeremiah's knees crumpled, and the mud crept higher. The circle of light above turned purple-blue and then black. Jeremiah dozed.

An urgent whisper woke him. "Jeremiah!"

"God?" Jeremiah's heart leaped. "I knew You would come."

A shaky, very human voice answered, "Be quiet, and slip this cloth under your arms. We're pulling you out."

A cloth sling was lowered into the muck beside him. With stiff fingers Jeremiah put the sling in place and felt himself being pulled from the mud, up, up along the rock walls until he finally fell out onto the courtyard floor.

Dark figures stripped off his wet robes, dried him, and helped him to dress in warm clothing. "Now come." He was pulled to his feet. "His Majesty King Zedekiah wants to see you."

Hope swept through Jeremiah. His stiff legs danced as he followed the men through the Temple yard. If the king had saved his life and wanted to see him, it meant Zedekiah had changed his mind. He was ready to end the war, to surrender to the Babylonians and save his people.

Jeremiah's bright hope faded when he was brought into a small room lit by one small lamp. He found the king slumped on a bench. Zedekiah's eyes were sunk deep into his head, and his plump cheeks sagged limply over his tangled beard. "Jeremiah," he whispered and reached up to clutch the prophet's robe, "I'm scared. We're losing the war. Tell me what to do. What does God want me to do?"

Jeremiah straightened up and filled his voice with all the power and faith he felt in God. He knew this was his last chance. He had to convey God's message to the frightened king tonight. He had to give him the strength to oppose the war party that had dragged the king into this hopeless war.

"God asks only that you should live by the laws of the Torah, not that you should be a powerful king over an independent Judah. The war with Babylonia is a terrible mistake. This is what the God of Israel says: 'If you will go out (surrender) to the princes of Babylonia, your soul will live, your family will be saved, and this city will not be destroyed by fire. If you will not go out, the city will be burned and neither you nor your family will be saved!'"

Zedekiah blinked, as if the lamp's flame were too bright. With trembling lips he said, "B-but there are people in the camp of the Babylonians who want to kill me. I'm afraid to surrender."

"Obey God, and you'll be safe," Jeremiah advised urgently.

But Zedekiah bowed his head and covered his face with clenched fists. "Don't tell anybody what we spoke about here, please," he mumbled.

I've lost, thought the prophet as he was led back to the court of the guards. Every bone in his body ached, and he was filled with the misery he had felt in the dark pit. I've lost. The king is more afraid of the war party than he is of God. There will be no surrender. The city will burn.

All the next day Jeremiah sat silently and hopelessly on a goatskin in the corner of the yard. Around him soldiers tightened their bow strings and sharpened their swords, preparing for battle. Jeremiah ignored them. He was already mourning for the dying city of Jerusalem.

In the evening a soldier poked him with his sword hilt. "You've got a visitor," he growled. Jeremiah's youngest cousin, curly-haired, freckled Hanamel stood timidly by the gate. "My father sent me here from Anatot to bring you this," he said, and handed a scroll to Jeremiah. "My father asks that you buy his fields in Anatot. This is the deed to the land."

The guards roared with laughter. "Jeremiah, you're crazy!" shouted the captain. "You rant and rave that the Babylonians will destroy us, and now you want to buy a field? What for? If your prophecy comes true, God forbid, the land will be Babylonian."

"He's not crazy. He's a traitor," growled another soldier. "He loves the Babylonians, and they love him. We should have left him in the pit to die!" His hate-filled eyes glared at Jeremiah from under his helmet, and he raised his sword threateningly. "Leave him be!" the captain ordered. "The king wants him alive."

The tension in the yard was so thick, Jeremiah could hardly breathe. Hanamel pressed close to him, afraid of the angry soldiers. Jeremiah smelled the fragrance of fig trees and vineyards on his rough shirt. Oh, God, why am I here, alone and hated, when I could have lived my life peacefully in Anatot? he thought.

He took the scroll, unrolled it, and read, BUY MY FIELD THAT IS IN ANATOT. IT IS YOUR INHERITANCE.

Inheritance? He shook his head and thought bitterly, Has my uncle gone crazy? What will be left of Anatot after the Babylonians have finished with it? Jeremiah began to roll up the scroll again, but the last words would not disappear: IT IS YOUR INHERITANCE. They shimmered inside his eyes like the bright image of the sun after he had looked at it too long. And slowly he began to understand. The scroll was not only a message from his uncle–it was also a message from God. God was making a promise that the inheritance of Israel would not be lost. The battle with Babylonia would be lost. Jerusalem would be destroyed. But one day the people of Israel would regain their inheritance.

"'Houses, fields, and vineyards shall be bought again in this land,' says God. That is the message of the field in Anatot," murmured Jeremiah. "It is our inheritance." A wave of strength swept through his starved body. He pulled himself up to stand and shouted at the surprised soldiers, "We will live! We will inherit this land again!" He kissed the scroll, and then he kissed his young cousin on both cheeks. "Tell your father he's made a sale!" he cried.

Writings

Jeremiah watched helplessly as the king of Judah led his people into the final battle against Babylonia. He knew they would lose. The Temple would be destroyed, the city would be plundered, and the Jews would be dragged into exile to become slaves and servants for their enemies. Jeremiah sat and mourned and wrote these lines:

> How does the city sit alone that was full of people.
>
> How has she become like a widow–she that was great among the nations and princess among the provinces–how has she become a slave!
>
> She weeps bitterly in the night and her tears are on her cheeks.
>
> Among all her lovers she has none to comfort her. . . .
>
> All her friends . . . have become her enemies.

Lamentations 1:1-2 (attributed to Jeremiah)

With farseeing prophet's eyes Jeremiah saw a better time coming. The Jewish people would not die in exile. They would live on and grow strong in lands far away from their beloved Land of Israel:

> Thus says the God of Israel to all who are carried away as captives:
>
> Build houses and live in them. Plant gardens and eat their fruit.
>
> Take wives and beget sons and daughters. And take wives for your sons and give your daughters to husbands, so they may have children and your numbers may increase, not become fewer. And seek the peace of the city into which I have caused you to be carried as captives.
>
> And pray to the Lord for it, because in its peace you shall have peace."

Jeremiah 29:4-7

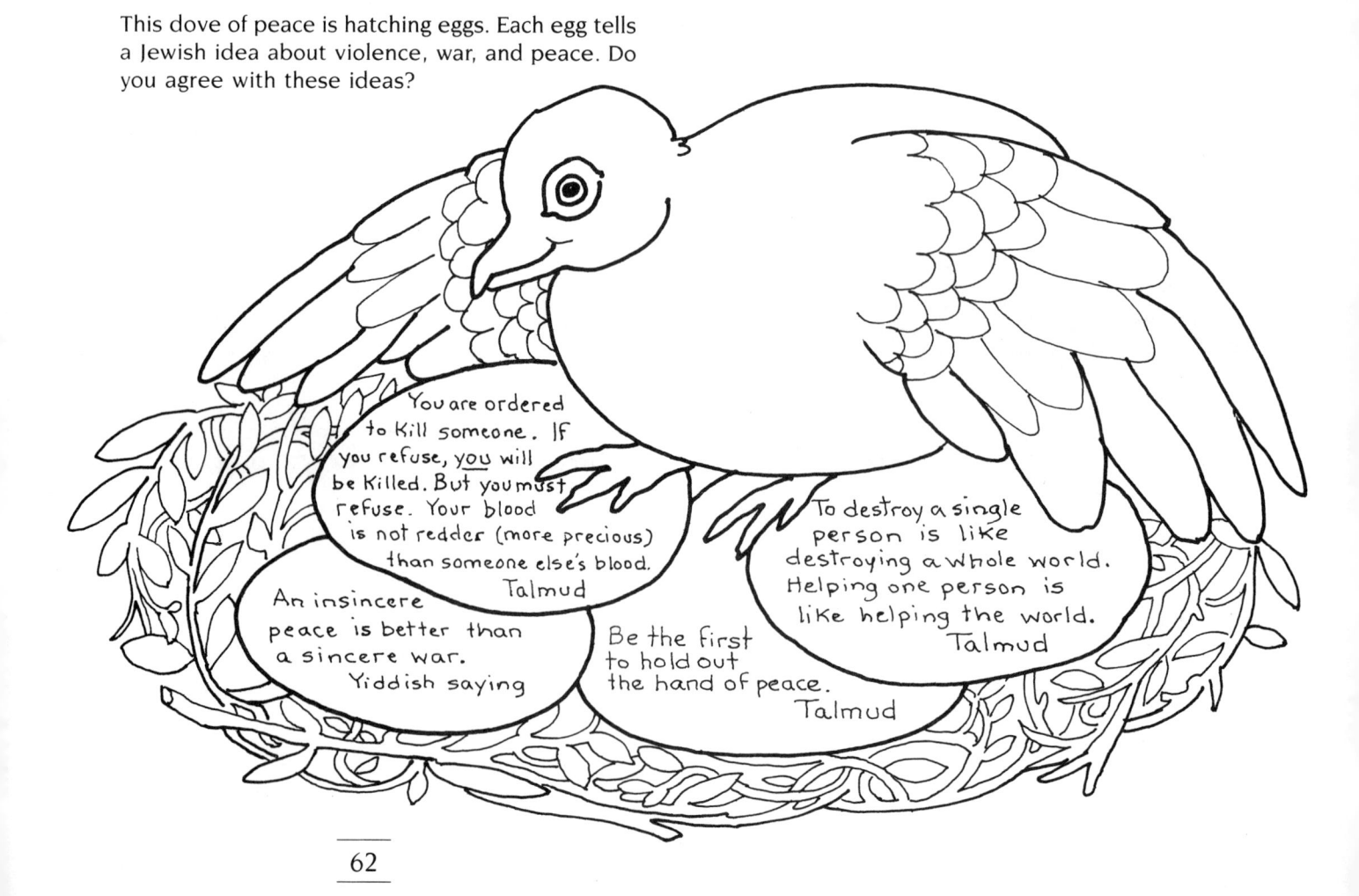

This dove of peace is hatching eggs. Each egg tells a Jewish idea about violence, war, and peace. Do you agree with these ideas?

- You are ordered to kill someone. If you refuse, you will be killed. But you must refuse. Your blood is not redder (more precious) than someone else's blood. —Talmud
- An insincere peace is better than a sincere war. —Yiddish saying
- Be the first to hold out the hand of peace. —Talmud
- To destroy a single person is like destroying a whole world. Helping one person is like helping the world. —Talmud

JEREMIAH WORD JUMBLE

Think of the word that explains each phrase below. Find it in the jumble of letters. The words go horizontally, vertically, and diagonally. Circle each word.
For example–the king of Judah, Zedekiah, is already circled.
King of Judah
Capital city of Judah
Enemy nation
God's law
Jeremiah's home town
Jeremiah was against war and for _____.
House of worship built by Solomon
Hebrew name for Solomon's house of worship
Jeremiah's cousin
Book of the Bible written by Jeremiah
Two bad names that people called Jeremiah
Jews are called the Children of _____.
Zedekiah ruled over _____.
Jeremiah was thrown into a _____ with _____ at the bottom.

```
L O Z E D E K I A H
A B A B Y L O N I A
M H N P I T M U P T
E P A I S R U L E R
N O T N R I D H A A
T T O R A H V A C I
A H T T E M P L E T
T R A V L I E R Y O
I B E T O N E L E R
O H A M I K D A S H
N J E R U S A L E M
S J U D A H L I A R
```

Check your answers on page 80.

A SAD PROPHET

Jeremiah was a sad prophet for two reasons:
1. He saw the realm of Judah destroyed.
2. He was called "traitor" and was hated by his own people because he tried to stop the war.

It would have been easy to be quiet and to go along with the war party, but God and his conscience would not let him be quiet.
Think of two times when you disagreed with your friends about something important.

1.

2.

Did you tell your friends that you disagreed? _____ yes _____ no

Did you go along with the majority? _____ yes _____ no

What should you have done? _____

After the time of Jeremiah the Jews lost their land and their army. Like the Jew in the following story they had to learn to talk their way out of trouble rather than to fight.

Two enemy armies faced each other across no-man's-land. The general shouted, "Get ready to attack! It will be man against man in hand-to-hand combat!" "P-please, sir," called the new Jewish recruit, "would you show me my man? Maybe I can come to an agreement with him."

63

7. EZEKIEL

The story goes on. . . .

While Jeremiah watched the struggle of the doomed city of Jerusalem, another prophet was bringing God's message to the Jewish exiles in Babylonia. The prophet Ezekiel had been carried off with other Jewish captives after an earlier Babylonian victory over Judah. Now they lived in exile in a city called Tel Aviv, in Babylonia. It wasn't a bad life, but the Jews were lonely for their own land and their Temple. More than anything else they wanted to go home again. What a thickheaded people, thought Ezekiel; they are unhappy because they are in exile. But God sent them into exile because they were violent and rebellious. So why haven't they learned their lesson? Why are they still violent and rebellious? I have to make them listen. I have to hammer some sense into their heads before it's too late. Ezekiel tugged at his unruly beard and thought and thought and came up with some wild ideas.

THE BEST SHOW IN TOWN

At first nobody in Tel Aviv believed Ezekiel the priest. He told wild unbelievable stories and did crazy things that embarrassed the Judeans and made their Babylonian neighbors laugh out loud. For instance, one morning he came racing to the town well with his hair and beard flying wildly in all directions and his eyes popping with excitement.

"I've seen God!" he yelled. "I was sitting on the riverbank and I looked up, and there was God sitting on a great throne—"

Nissan the baker stopped loading water jugs on his donkey. "Oh, yeah," he jeered, "I looked up one day and saw my grandmother sitting on a donkey."

The villagers waiting to fill their jugs laughed. But laughter never stopped Ezekiel. He rushed to tell his vision. "Listen," he cried, "the heavens opened above me, and a blazing fire flared out. Four weird creatures came through the flames. They had huge wings and faces that flashed like lightning. Each face had four sides. One side was a man, another side was an ox, another a lion, and the last an eagle. The creatures rolled across the sky on giant wheels with a noise as loud as a marching army!"

"Eight faces, wings, and wheels? Better lay off the wine, Ezekiel.

That's where your creatures come from–right out of the wine jug," Nissan teased him.

Ezekiel pressed on. "No, listen, here's the most important part. Suddenly I heard a voice from the sky above the creatures. I looked up and saw a jeweled throne with a glowing being sitting on it. The being glowed like a rainbow shining out of storm clouds. Then it spoke and said, 'Son of man, I am sending you to the Children of Israel to warn them to worship Me and follow My Torah. If they disobey, I will punish them. I will scatter them to the winds.'"

Nissan's round, red face turned grim. "Cut that out!" he growled. "We don't need to hear that 'punishment' stuff. We've already been scattered. That's why we're here in Babylonia, in exile."

"Why do you always say nasty things, Ezekiel," complained one of the women. "Other prophets say nice things."

"How I wish I could," Ezekiel answered sadly. "But I can only say the words God puts into my mouth."

Shaking her head, the woman turned away and lowered the pail into the well. Nissan kicked his donkey disgustedly and clattered off to the bakery. But some of the others stood quietly, dreamy-eyed, as if they were still seeing the four flaming creatures and the rainbow figure of God.

A few days later Ezekiel staggered into the marketplace carrying a load of bricks.

"Hey, Zeke," roared Yoni the fish seller, "are you giving up the prophet business? Want to be a bricklayer?"

Without a word Ezekiel squatted and arranged the bricks to form a model of a city wall. He set sticks against the wall as tiny battering rams and piled earth ramps to reach the top of the wall, as if an enemy were preparing to charge up and take the city. And around the outside he built a camp filled with tiny enemy soldiers.

Children came to watch the prophet work. "Is it a game?" they asked. "Can we play?"

The prophet shook his head, and they ran away. Only one older girl stayed. Finally she asked, "Is the city our own Jerusalem?"

He nodded.

"Will it fall to the enemy?"

He nodded again. The girl's eyes filled with tears, and she walked slowly away.

When Ezekiel finished building his model, he lay down on the earth beside the tiny city. And then he felt God's warning words pushing, pushing inside him. He knew he had to speak out again even though people were angry at him. "This city will fall to the Babylonians," he cried. "The people of Israel will be driven out of their own land to wander hungry and thirsty in strange lands."

Day after day Ezekiel lay on the earth beside the model of Jerusalem. Dogs stopped to sniff at him. People walked past and asked, "Is he sick?" "Is he crazy?" The girl put a robe over him to keep him warm. Nissan the baker squatted beside him for a while, bringing flat bread, warm from the oven. But Ezekiel turned his head away. He ate only the tiny bread ration that God had allowed him.

"Why do you say such awful things, Zeke?" Nissan asked. "You know God won't let Jerusalem be destroyed. It's God's city. The Temple stands there."

Ezekiel shook his head. "The Temple will be destroyed," he repeated.

The oldest priest of the town came to sit with Ezekiel. His white beard trembled as he said, "My son, you're making everybody very nervous. If we lose Jerusalem and the Temple, we'll have nothing to believe in anymore. Have pity, and don't say such terrible things. Please get up, go home, have a good meal."

"The people ought to be nervous," said Ezekiel. "They are violent with one another, and they rebel against God's laws. The Temple will fall!"

More and more people came to sit with Ezekiel. Many argued with him, a few prayed, and some stared anxiously at the model of the city they loved so much. But one morning when they came, Ezekiel was gone. He had walked away from his model of Jerusalem.

Nissan hurried past on his way to work. "Aha, so he's done playing," he exclaimed. "What a faker!" He kicked the bricks and scattered them. Just then a little boy ran into the square. "Ezekiel is doing something new," he squeaked excitedly. "Come and see."

Nissan put down his basket of grain and ran to the prophet's mud brick house. A crowd of people, goats, and a few chickens were standing around, watching to see what Ezekiel would do next. The people gasped as the prophet raised a sharp, shiny razor. He began to hack at his wild beard and his long shaggy hair. He cut and cut until there was a pile of hair on the grindstone before him. He divided the pile into three parts. With a burning stick he set fire to one pile.

"These are the people of Israel," he cried. "One third of Israel will burn!" A smell like burning chicken feathers filled the air. The children held their noses.

Ezekiel raised the second pile high and flung it into the air. "One third of Israel will be scattered to the wind!"

Then he snatched up the razor and began to chop at the last third. "One third of Israel will die by the sword!" he shouted.

"Liar!" screamed Nissan, and rushed at Ezekiel with fists clenched. His neighbors held him back, but they, too, shouted, "Liar, traitor, you want to destroy us!"

Ezekiel put his hands to his ears and outshouted them. "'Because you haven't followed My laws I am against you,' says God, 'I will punish you before the eyes of all the nations.'"

"No, no! Liar! Fool!" People waved and yelled until they were hoarse and finally turned their backs and left Ezekiel standing alone over his pile of smoking hair.

When the heat of day had passed, there was a noisy meeting of the elders in the yard of the flour mill. "How long can we let this lunatic babble? He's worrying people," Nissan complained.

"He is a priest and a prophet. He has a right to speak," answered a priest.

"Who says he's a prophet? Other prophets don't shout about doom and chop off their hair!" cried Yoni the fish seller.

And Noah the merchant proclaimed, "The man is a disgrace to the community. He makes the Babylonians laugh at us. We have to shut him up."

The argument stopped when the elders heard hooves pounding on the desert road. A few minutes later a sweating horse and rider clattered into the marketplace, and they heard shouts and cries. "Jerusalem has fallen, Jerusalem has fallen!" the rider called hoarsely. "The Temple is in flames!"

Ezekiel sat on the hard earth of his courtyard with his head bowed. Around him other exiled Judeans sat crying and praying. Their heads were covered with gray ashes as a sign of mourning. Nissan came to Ezekiel with red, tear-filled eyes. "You were right," he said. "I believe you now, but it's too late. We're lost in a strange land with no home, no Jerusalem to go back to. How can we be Jews here in Babylonia? How can we bring sacrifices and pray without our Temple?"

For once Ezekiel had no answer. He put his hand on Nissan's shoulder, and they sat together with tears running down their cheeks.

After a while Noah the merchant blew his nose, sniffed, and looked around. Then he stretched his cramped legs and stood up. "Ahem." He cleared his throat. "Ahem–fellow Judeans, listen to me."

A few sad faces looked up.

"You all know me. I'm a hardheaded businessman, and I'm not afraid to face the facts. Now, as I see it, this is a fact–the Hebrew God lost the war! God was too weak to protect Jerusalem and the Temple. So the God of Judah is a loser. I think it's time to switch to a winner like the Babylonian god Marduk."

Everybody was listening now with shocked, angry faces.

"But Marduk is just an idol made of wood. How can we worship him?" asked an old woman.

Noah argued, "Marduk's people won the war. That proves he's good for something. I say go with the winner! We're in Marduk's country now, not in God's country."

"No! You have it all wrong." Nissan stood up and faced the merchant. Our God is not weak. God let Jerusalem and the Temple be destroyed because of us, because we didn't deserve God's help and protection."

"That's right," others called out. "Idols are pieces of wood and stone shaped by human beings. God is everyplace, not only in the Land of Israel!"

Ezekiel sat quietly and listened as his neighbors argued. He was sad for them but so proud of their faith in God. "Are You listening, God?" he whispered, and wiggled a finger at the sky. "Do You hear how loyal they are?"

The arguing grew angrier and louder until at last Noah was shouted down. He clutched his embroidered robe to his chest and stormed out of the courtyard yelling, "Losers–you're all losers! You'll be sorry!"

The others sat down again to pray and mourn.

"God, God," Ezekiel begged silently, "how can You abandon such a loyal people?"

Suddenly Ezekiel felt an answer to his plea. He felt himself being lifted out of the gray, shadowy courtyard. High above the mud-colored houses and fine shrines of Tel Aviv he was carried, and on across the grim, rocky desert. Beyond the desert he saw a sunny mountaintop. A large, gleaming building stood on it. This is the Land of Israel, thought Ezekiel with wonder as he floated down and stood in the soft grass beside the building. A man holding a measuring rod stood waiting for him. "This building is the house of God," said the man. "I will show you how it must be built. Then you will go back to your people and teach them."

The man led Ezekiel through the building and gave him exact instructions about how to build every wall, courtyard, and room in this new house of God. And as they walked, a great light began to fill the building. Even the earth around it began to glow. A voice like the rushing of waters spoke to them and said, "I am God who caused My people to be led into exile. Now I will gather them to their own land. And I will live with the Children of Israel forever."

The light faded. The green hilltop and the building disappeared. Suddenly Ezekiel was back in the shadowy courtyard with his bottom numb from sitting. Around him the Judeans still sat sobbing, rocking back and forth, and praying.

"Listen, my people!" he cried joyously. "Sweep the ashes from your heads! I've seen God, and God is with us. We will live according to the Torah, and God will gather us out of all the lands of exile and bring us home. And then we'll build a great Temple. And God showed me exactly how to do it. Look here. This is how we'll build it."

He ripped a twig from a fig branch that hung over the courtyard wall, leaned forward, and began to scratch the design of the Temple in the hard-packed earth. "Here in the middle is the Holy of Holies. It will be twenty cubits square and . . ."

Men and women rubbed away their tears and crowded around him. Children squeezed in between, anxious to see. And this time nobody laughed at Ezekiel the prophet, especially not Nissan.

Writings

Ezekiel painted pictures of the future with his words and his playacting. Sometimes they were pictures of death and punishment. Sometimes they were hopeful and happy and gave people the courage to face hard times. This prophecy of the "dry bones" was a great comfort to many. They believed that even if they died, or the whole people of Israel died, God would bring them back to life. Many centuries later black slaves were comforted by Ezekiel's words and sang them in a spiritual.

The hand of the Lord was upon me and carried me out . . . and set me down in the midst of a valley that was full of bones. . . . And God said to me, "Son of man, can these bones live?" And I answered, "O Lord God, only You can know." Again God said to me, "Prophesy over these bones and say to them: 'O dry bones, hear the word of the Lord. The Lord God says, Behold, I will cause breath to enter you, and you will live. And I will lay muscles on you, and flesh, and cover you with skin . . . and you will live. And you shall know that I am the Lord.'"

So I prophesied as I was commanded. And there was a noise, a rattling, and the bones came together–each bone to its bone. As I watched, the muscles and flesh came on them and the skin covered them. But there was no breath in them.

Then God said to me, "Prophesy . . . and say to the breath, 'Come with four winds, O breath, and breathe upon these dead so they may live.'" So I prophesied . . . and the breath came into them, and they lived and stood on their feet, a very great army. Then God said to me, "Son of man, these bones are the whole house of Israel. They say, 'Our bones are dried, and our hope is lost. We are cut off.' Prophesy and say to them, 'Thus says the Lord, My people, I will open your graves and bring you out and bring you into the Land of Israel. And you shall know that I am the Lord.'"

Ezekiel 37:1-13

MESSAGES

Ezekiel told of marvelous visions and did shocking things in order to make people listen to God's messages. How would you spread an important message? Make a speech at a shopping mall? Do a radio interview or a skit for TV?

Think of an important message your class ought to hear. You can take a stand *for* or *against* one of the following topics, or choose one of your own:
- Cheating on tests teaches cooperation.
- Dress codes are undemocratic.
- Chanukah and Christmas should be celebrated at school.
- Stop wasting natural resources.

1. Write an advertising jingle to spread your message.
2. Paint a poster or a sandwich board to carry around the classroom.
3. Think of another gimmick.

EZEKIEL'S WORD MATCH

Draw a line from the word in Column A to the related word in Column B

A	B
1. Tel Aviv	1. prophet in Judah
2. Jeremiah	2. Temple
3. Marduk	3. three piles of hair
4. happy prophecy	4. wood and stone
5. Holy of Holies	5. dry bones will live
6. Ezekiel	6. Jerusalem
7. God's city	7. Babylonian god
8. idols	8. prophet in Babylonia
9. gloomy prophecy	9. Babylonian city

Check your answers on page 80.

ROLLING HOME

During the long exile from the Land of Israel many Jews continued to believe that, when the Messiah came, God would raise their bones and carry them to Israel. But they were afraid the bones would have to roll over mountains and under oceans to reach their homeland. Some careful old people packed up and came to the land to die so as to spare their bones the long roll.

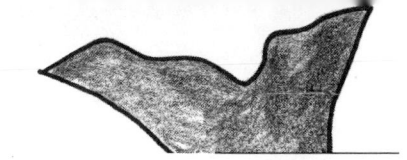

A LIGHT UNTO THE NATIONS   8.

Toward the end of the time of the prophets two men brought a new and difficult message to the people of Israel. They said Jews must do more than watch their own behavior; they must also show other people how to behave kindly.

The story goes on....

Jonah, the first of the two men, didn't like this message at all. When God called him to warn the people of Nineveh to change their wicked ways, Jonah tried to run away and hide. But God caught up with him and had him thrown into the sea, swallowed by a whale, and then tossed out again. Finally Jonah had to follow orders and go to Nineveh. But he wasn't happy about it. What do I care about the people of Nineveh! he thought. God decided to teach the prophet a lesson. One hot day God raised a plant to grow and shade Jonah from the burning sun. The next day God sent a worm to kill the plant. Jonah sat baking in the sun and wished he could die. And God said to him, "You are concerned about a plant you didn't labor over, that came up in one night and died the next night. Why shouldn't I be concerned for the great city of Nineveh with its 120,000 people who don't know their left hand from their right?" (Jonah 4:10-11)

The prophet known as the Second Isaiah didn't need to be swallowed by a whale before he would speak the words of God. He delivered the message willingly. The people of Judah had been driven out of their land and lived in Babylonia when they heard the words of the Second Isaiah. He comforted them and promised that their religion would serve not only the Jewish people but all the people of the world. "My house is a house of prayer for all people," God said, in the words of the Second Isaiah (Isaiah 56:7). Then God laid a big responsibility on the Jewish people: God told them they must be an example of a good, righteous way of life to all the people of the world:

> It is not enough that you should be My servant to raise up the tribes of Jacob and to restore the people of Israel. I will also make you a light unto the nations, so that My salvation may reach to the ends of the earth.
>
> Isaiah 49:6

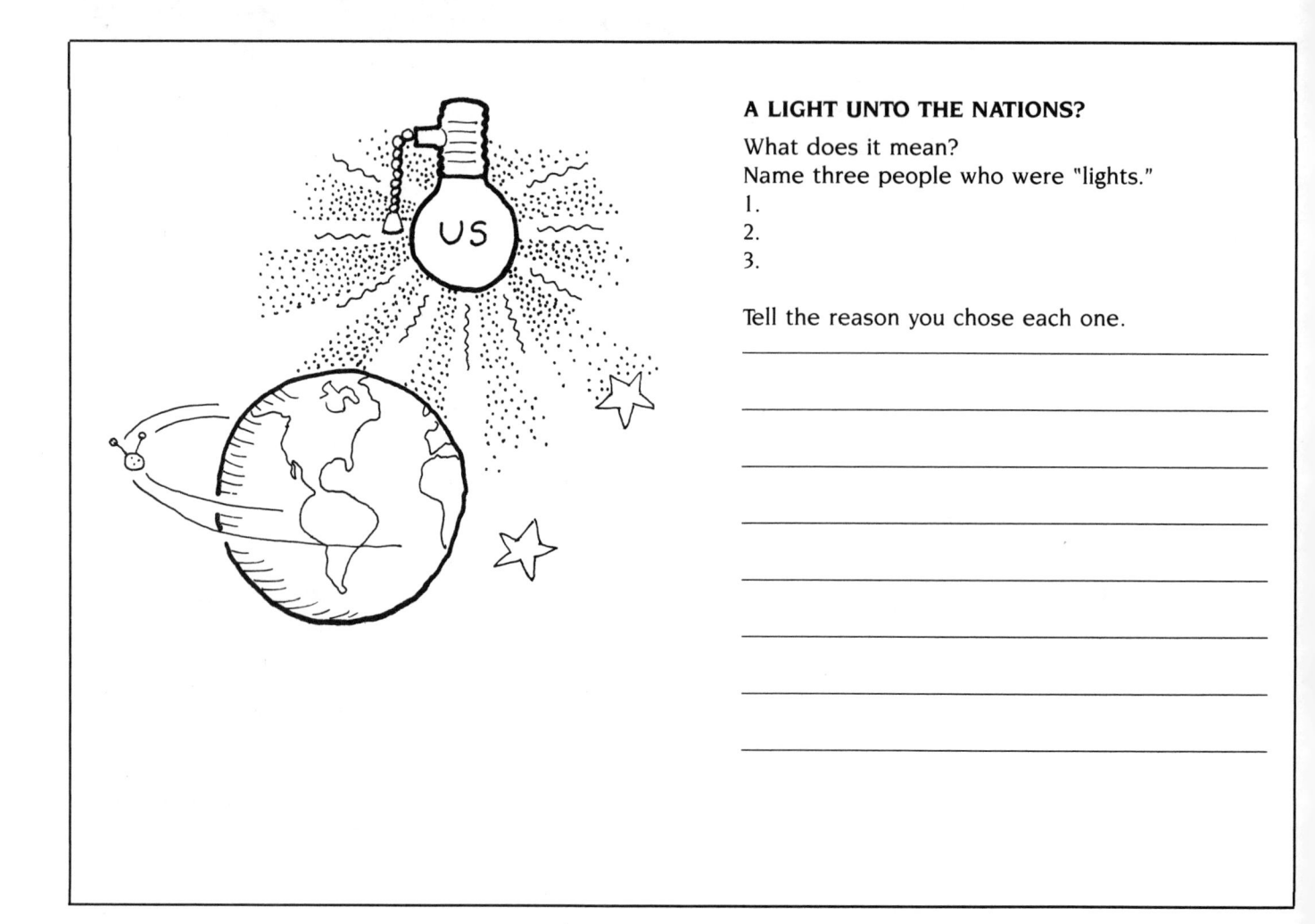

A LIGHT UNTO THE NATIONS?

What does it mean?
Name three people who were "lights."
1.
2.
3.

Tell the reason you chose each one.

CIRCLES OF RESPONSIBILITY

From the beginning God made the Jews responsible to follow the laws of the Torah. At first people only felt responsible for Temple worship and sacrifices. As time passed the circle of responsibility grew larger.

Circle One:

The first prophets pulled the Jewish people together into a tight circle–the nation. And they taught the Jews to worship and sacrifice to one God.

Circle Two:

Later prophets made a larger circle. They stressed fairness and justice between people even more than worship and sacrifice in the Temple.

Circle Three:

The last prophets saw the Jews lose their Temple and scatter throughout the world. Now the circle grew larger. It included many other nations. Be just, study Torah, and be a light unto the nations, the prophets instructed the Jews, and you will bring peace to the world.

GROWING UP HAPPENS IN CIRCLES, TOO

Babies live in a tiny circle of infant and parents. Soon the circle grows to include the whole family and then the neighborhood. In time more and more circles form. Fill in these circles to show where friends, religious school and synagogue, the country, Israel, the world, and other important elements fit around the center–YOU. Pick two or three of the places or people in the circles, and think of what your responsibility is toward them.

9. THEN AND NOW

The people of Judea were driven out of their land and carried off to Babylonia more than 2,500 years ago. When the Babylonian exile began, the time of the great prophets of Israel ended. For 800 years they had nagged and scolded, taught and threatened. During that time the lives of the Jewish people seesawed up and down, from weakness to strength and back to weakness.

They started out as a frightened bunch of ex-slaves wandering in the desert. Moses brought them the Torah, taught them to believe in one God, to love the Land of Israel, and to take care of one another. By Dvora's time the Hebrew tribes had drifted apart, but she forced them to unite and fight for one another. When they were tempted to worship comfortable gods they could see and touch, the prophets Samuel and Elijah forced them back to their stern, invisible God and to the Ark of the Covenant.

Even when the seesaw rose high in the air–when the realms of Israel and Judah were strong and independent–prophets like Isaiah could not sit back and be yes-men. They said no to the bossy behavior of kings and noblemen. "You can't pay God off with sweet-smelling sacrifices," they said. "You have to be honest and just."

When the seesaw dropped, when the realm of Judah was destroyed, the prophets Jeremiah and Ezekiel cried along with their people. Then they made a hopeful promise. Though the Temple was gone and sacrifices could no longer be made, God and the Torah would stay with the Jewish people. They would always be with them, wherever the people went. And one day the people of Israel would return to the Land of Israel.

The best and toughest promise came at the end of the time of the prophets. The Second Isaiah told the Jewish people they would become messengers of God. They would be a "light unto the nations," bringing God's Torah to the whole world.

Each prophet had to deal with the problems of his or her own time. Sometimes their messages were very different. Dvora pulled the people to fight a war, but Jeremiah argued that the king must surrender to the enemy rather than fight a war. The messages of Elijah and Jonah were very different, too. Elijah cared only about the Jews and fought fiercely to drive idol worshipers out of the Land of Israel. But Jonah learned, in spite of himself, that he must care about all people–Jews and non-Jews alike.

Today, as in Elijah's time, there are many Jews who know nothing about God and the Torah. Today, as in Amos's and Isaiah's time, there are poor, hungry people as well as selfish or dishonest people who take advantage of others. Today, as in Jeremiah's time, there are unnecessary wars.

And today we face new problems that the prophets never met, such as pollution, overpopulation, and the squandering of natural resources. Would it help us to solve all the old and new problems if Ezekiel or Elijah suddenly stood up in our biggest shopping mall and told us what to do? It probably wouldn't help. People might not listen, at least not right away.

The messages of the prophets were not heard right away in their own time either. But they became an important influence in Jewish life in the 2,500 years that followed, right up to today. They influenced other great religions, too. Christianity and Islam (the Muslim religion) both were guided by the Hebrew prophets.

Here are some of the ways the words of the prophets helped Jews over the centuries:

- When the Jews found themselves exiled to strange lands, Jeremiah's words reminded them they could pray and live according to God's rules anyplace in the world.
- Long before the enactment of social welfare laws, Jewish communities obeyed the words of prophets like Amos and took care of their poor and their sick. They even set up public funds to provide dowries for orphan girls and pooled their money to pay ransoms for captive Jews.
- Jews became leaders in fights against oppression–just as the Second Isaiah would have wished. In Russia they led the struggle to overthrow a cruel czar. In the United States they helped organize labor unions and later became leaders in the civil rights movement.
- When the Land of Israel began to be rebuilt as a Jewish homeland, Jews from all over the world remembered God's promises as told by Moses, Ezekiel, and Jeremiah and rushed to return to the Promised Land.

During their lifetimes the prophets demanded so much! They criticized, and argued, and quarreled. They were noisy neighbors and demanding friends. They insisted that being a Jew was not a condition, like being skinny or blue-eyed or bald; being a Jew was a job people had to work at, to try harder to live responsible lives. They often made the people of their time feel guilty and angry. Sometimes, even today, they make people feel guilty. It's not easy to be a "light unto the nations." But the prophets were driven by God. They didn't know how to make things easy—either for themselves or anybody else. Like a good coach or teacher they set high standards for their people, standards we are still trying to achieve.

FROM HAND TO HAND

The Talmud tells us Moses received the Torah from Mount Sinai and handed it on to Joshua, Joshua to the Elders, the Elders to the Prophets, and the Prophets to the Men of the Great Assembly.

The Great Assembly handed the Torah to our ancestors. They handed it from generation to generation until it reached us here today. Torah is the basis of Jewish customs and beliefs. What Jewish customs and beliefs have you learned from your family and at religious school? List five.

1.

2.

3.

4.

5.

Which seem most important to you—important enough to hand on to your children?

A Message From Space

Pretend you are a modern prophet. You suddenly have the chance to speak to the whole world via satellite. What will you say? Write your message on the lines in the box.

WORKBOOK ANSWERS

The three books of Torah, page 17.
1. Torah
2. Prophets
3. Writings

1. תּוֹרָה
2. נְבִיאִים
3. כְּתוּבִים

Dvora's victory song, page 26.
1. The enemy persecuted travelers and villagers. "Travelers went on back roads, and villagers ran away from their villages."
2. No. "Curse those who did not come to help God."
3. Dvora said, "The highways were empty... until I, Dvora, arose." Proud or truthful? What do you think?
4. "To every man a girl or two. To Sisera brightly colored clothing...."

A Dvora crossword puzzle, page 27.

Samuel's scrambled words, page 35.
1. chariot
2. priest
3. altar
4. commandments
5. Philistine

Long live King "What's-His-Name," page 36.
SAUL

Jeremiah word jumble, page 63.

Ezekiel's word match, page 72.

A	B
1	9
2	1
3	7
4	5
5	2
6	8
7	6
8	4
9	3

80

DATES

The prophets lived before the common era (B.C.E.).
Add 2,000 to each date to figure out how long ago the person lived.

1900 B.C.E. Abraham and his family came to Israel.
1750 B.C.E. Abraham's descendants (the Hebrews) moved to Egypt.
1450 B.C.E. Moses led the Hebrews from Egypt to Israel.
1200 B.C.E. Dvora battled the Canaanites.
1050 B.C.E. Samuel led the Hebrews.
 850 B.C.E. Elijah fought for one God.
 700 B.C.E. Isaiah demanded justice.
 600 B.C.E. Jeremiah warned of defeat.
 600 B.C.E. Ezekiel brought hope.
 550 B.C.E. The Second Isaiah set a high

BJE/RMC